My Gonads Roar

# My Gonads Roar

The twisted world of anagrams
– from pop idols to celebrity chefs

## RICHARD NAPIER

First published in 2008
by Faber and Faber Limited
3 Queen Square London WC1N 3AU

Typeset by Faber and Faber Limited
Printed and bound in the UK by
CPI Mackays, Chatham ME5 8TD

A CIP record for this book
is available from the British Library

ISBN: 978–0–571–24394–5

2 4 6 8 10 9 7 5 3 1

To Perky Meatbal
**The Vole of my File**

# Contents

# COD
# NUTRITION

(That's *Introduction* by way of introduction)

I love anagrams. Always have done. From the day my mum first taught me the intricacies of the *Daily Telegraph* crossword, to the drunken evening I worked out that ex-footballer and professional Frenchman **David Ginola** became *Vagina Dildo*, wordplay has intrigued and continually surprised me. (For those of you that haven't yet realised, *My Gonads Roar* is an anagram of **Gordon Ramsay**. There'll be a lot of this sort of thing, so if you're finding it tough going already, you might want to put this down and go see what about the French has annoyed Jeremy Clarkson this Christmas.)

Anagrams have been around for thousands of years. Since Adam and Eve first figured out that *repents* is an anagram of serpent, people have been fascinated by the little ironies that occur when you begin to play with the order of a word's letters. Pythagoras and Plato were both said to have been big anagram fans – in ancient Greek, obviously, so not particularly quotable – and various Jewish mystics in the thirteenth century, particularly the Kabbalists, were big on saying stuff like 'Secret mysteries are woven into the numbers of letters'. Famously, Louis XIII once appointed a Royal Anagrammatist to entertain his court with amusing anagrams of people's names. Maybe there'll be work for me when Charlie takes over from Liz.

Most recently, of course, it has been Dan Brown who has carried the anagram beacon into the dark recesses of popular culture. This book has roughly one hundred times more anagrams in it than his record-breaking bestseller, which made him a millionaire many times over. I'll leave you to do the maths.

As a seasoned anagrammatist, I see word alternatives all the time. Like the kid in that film, but with anagrams not dead people. I can't see something without changing its letters. Sitting in traffic behind a Cavalier, I'd think what *A Vile Car*. Indeed, my obsession meant that one year, I scared my own children when I wrote them a note saying that if they were good, *Satan* would come down the chimney. I've even written my own epitaph in anticipation of the day I meet my *Dog* – 'Even if I am *hated* in *death*, have *real fun* at my *funeral*.'

If I were an examiner, job interviewer or emperor of the world, I would start every test with the question, 'Name me two fruits that are anagrams of each other.' The question requires thought, imagination and creativity, and therefore gives you an immediate insight into the intelligence and flexibility of the candidate.

If you aren't able to work the answer out now, I hope you will by the end of the book. If, however, having finished the last page, you are still desperately shuffling the letters of coconut around, frantically checking the dictionary for the existence of the *cuntcoo*, you may have a way to go. Perhaps the joy I find in anagrams comes from the fact that nothing is added or indeed taken away. The new word is already there in the old one; you just can't see it yet, and because of this, anagrams always have a kind of truth about them.

Anagrams contain, for me, the essence of humour, that moment of surprise, of violent realignment that the simplest, funniest jokes have. They are utterly irreverent; they care little for reputations, and everything and everyone can be anagrammatised – celebrities in the worlds of sport, music, politics, books and films all get the treatment in the pages that follow.

The results are funny and occasionally crude, and often reveal something we've always suspected but have been afraid to think.

Is the new **Arctic Monkeys** album really going to be called *Sticky Romance*? Is there an Oscar for **Meg Ryan** for her role in the Nazi blockbuster *Germany*? And really, was ex-Manchester United coach **Steve McClaren** the *Cleverest Man(c)* for England?

So consider this book your anagram school. Interspersed with my own satirical look at the world is a series of tests on subjects ranging from The Royal Family to Countries and History. We'll start, though, with music and the home of *Farters of Arse – Greatest Shit.*

# Music

The cosmetic nature of names is, perhaps, more crucial in the music industry than any other. This is why budding artists spend an enormous amount of time inventing band names, noms de plume and pseudonyms, seeking to infuse an effortless cool into the very fabric of their name.

It was a stroke of genius that launched the **Spice Girls** into the pop world, as opposed to the *Pig Slicers*, although horses for courses and all that; and **Tears for Fears** would never have lasted beyond 'Mad World' had they debuted as *Farters of Arse*. Rumours that **the Backstreet Boys** are reinventing themselves as *Cheeky Tot Stabbers* are, alas, unfounded.

Paul Hewson, aka **Bono**, is another prime example. Would U2 be the band they are now, if fronted by a man called *Nobo*? I think not, although *Boon* might have squeezed a couple of top 40s out. Unfortunately for the Irish rock gods, anagrams know all of your secrets. Everything you are is revealed through rearrangement in Anagramland.

So how have other legends achieved their iconic status in our new alternative world? Well, **Belinda Carlisle** had *Ideal Brain Cells*, **Elvis Costello**'s *Voice Sells Lot*, **Bruce Springsteen** had a *Bursting Presence* and **Rod Stewart** made millions despite being the *Worst Dater*.

David **Essex** was more successful on that front as he always *Advised Sex*, as was **Axl Rose**, who guaranteed *Oral Sex*, along with **David Lee Roth**, *A Red-Hot Devil*, and **Alison Moyet**, *One Moist Lay*. **Simon Le Bon** has been less successful, however, after publicly admitting '*I Nob Melons*'. **Kylie Minogue** also needs to work on her somewhat bold chat-up line, '*You Like Minge?*' Apparently '*I Like 'Em Young*' is her excuse. Her sister **Danielle Minogue**'s qualities as a *Genuine Male Idol* are clear. But surely the best charades of all have been the sham weddings and attention-grabbing antics of **Britney Spears**, which were of course, the *Best PR in Years*.

The good news for **Chris Rea** is that he's a *Rich Arse*; less good news for **Sir Paul McCartney**, though – despite his *Musical Carpentry*, he was really taken to the cleaners by the *Mercenary Hatchet*, **Heather McCartney**.

Last word is from the lovely **George Michael**, whose comment on the subject is '*I Come, He Gargle.*' Thanks George.

In the seventies, a band called **Sad Café** released an album called *Façades*. Using their blueprint, here are some artists' names rearranged as the albums they could release and what those albums might be like.

**Arctic Monkeys** – STICKY ROMANCE

Thirteen teenage self-love anthems from the sprightly northerners, including 'Towel Stains', 'Sorry about the Tissues, Ma' and the smash hit single 'The Sheffield Spunker'.

## Mariah Carey – A HAIRY CREAM

Mariah Carey decides to dedicate a whole album to her new shaving foam sponsor. The songs 'Shaving All My Love', 'All I Want for Christmas is a Brazilian', 'Bic Me, Lick Me, Dick Me' and the epic 'Ballad of Baldy Beaver' really show off Mariah's extraordinary vocal range. The videos are fab, involving huge amounts of lather and the occasional Band-Aid.

## Barbra Streisand – SERBIAN BARSTARD

A far cry from 'The Way We Were', old Babs launches a vicious and indeed unwarranted attack on the Manchester United defender Nemanja Vidic. The single 'You're Not as Good in the Air as Rio' is particularly cutting.

## Pink Floyd – DINKY FLOP

Habitual concept-album splendour from the veterans of the deep and meaningful, this time tackling the tricky subject of male impotence. 'Say Goodbye to Mister Stiff', 'Droopy' and 'Are You In Yet?' will be the real stadium-pleasers.

## Red Hot Chili Peppers – DERELICT HIPHOPPERS

'Give it away, give it away, give it away now.' You know, sometimes I just wish they would. Nonsensical rapping and a lot of lisping.

## Chemical Brothers – BESMIRCH THE CAROL

A controversial alternative Christmas album from the big-beat fusion maestros, which includes 'O Little Town of Bethnal Green' and 'Ding Dong Merrily I'm High'.

## The Klaxons – LATEX HONKS

The Nu-Rave visionaries are back with an album consisting of the sound of someone wearing cheap latex trousers getting up from a sofa set to wicked wicked beats. Glowsticks are so in right now. If you're a twat.

## Céline Dion – NICE 'N' OILED

Céline takes a different direction with her seven-hundred-and-thirty-third release and it all gets a little inappropriate. Interesting album cover.

## Bruce Springsteen – BURPING ERECTNESS

A testosterone-belching and boning overload from Bruce Almighty sees him addressing such issues as impregnating young girls, getting blind drunk with the lads and driving fast American cars. In the soon-to-be-released single, 'Riding the Alcoholic Highway with My Baby', he manages to fit all three of his favourite subjects into four quite astonishing minutes.

## Christina Aguilera – CHILEAN AIR GUITARS

Filmed live in Santiago, Ms Aguilera literally gets her rocks off with some Red Hot Chileans. Her worldwide smash 'Dirrty' is performed with even more r's than normal, and the encore is unnecessarily messy.

## George Benson – GREEN BONGOES

George hits desperation stakes with a back-to-my-environmentalist-roots collection of drum and bass minus the bass nonsense. Dreadful. Really dreadful.

## Simon and Garfunkel – SANG FOUL IN DENMARK

As part of their reunion world tour, Paul and Art astonish crowds around the Little Mermaid statue with a hugely controversial set, which includes 'Get a Proper Flag', 'Hans Christian Who?', 'All Vikings are Gay' and 'Shove It up your Copenhagen'.

## Snow Patrol – POLAR TOWNS

Raising awareness of the melting caps as well as giving us another twelve songs that sound like, but aren't quite as good as, 'Run', come Ireland's much-loved indie rockers. Expect a video with a furry white bear on a slab of floating ice, whilst uncaring bastards in Knightsbridge drive one child around in a 4x4.

## Girls Aloud – SUGARDILLO

On this revolutionary album, the CD has actually
been replaced by a laminated A1 poster of the girls.
More importantly, what order do you have them in?
For me, anagram-wise, it has to be:

> One Nice Lady
> Harridan's Hag
> Nicer Bra Tools
> Killer Whambeys
> Hole Lyccer

## Alanis Morissette – MENSTRALITE OASIS

Alanis Morissette returns with forty-eight minutes of
twisted, revenge-filled, man-hating vitriol. With the
opening rockers 'Ballbreaker' and 'You Shithead',
the tone of the album is very much set. The lilting
ballad 'Touch Me There and I'll Kill You, Bollock
Brain' is an emotional tearjerker that will have your
lachrymal glands desperate for a refill. The entire
acidic vengeance climaxes with the toe-tapping,
reggae-tinged 'Gonna Turn Lezza'. A certainty for
the Mercury Music Prize shortlist.

## Amy Winehouse – WHY U SO MEANIE?

North London's most delicate wallflower just cannot understand why anyone would be against her. Let me think . . .

## Bryan Adams – RANDY SAMBA

In this 'Live in Rio' extravaganza, the old Cragmeister plays the crassly innuendo-ridden 'Summer of '69' three times during a tortuous two-hour live set in front of a worryingly enthusiastic Brazilian crowd. Watch them go, as well as throw, bananas when Big Bry announces, 'This is a song called "Everything I Do, I Do It for You, Rio".' Life-changing, in a male menopause sort of way.

## Bob Marley and the Wailers
### – BASEMENT HOLIDAY WARBLER

We're Jamming. Kingston.

## Stephen Gately – PLEASE THY GENT

Conflates biblical imagery from the Song of Solomon with the sort of squelchy, innuendo-laden beats not heard since 'Relax'. Meanwhile, Ronan Keating has the cold dead eyes of the walking damned.

## Simple Minds – MILD PENISMS

Stand-out tracks include 'Willy', 'Winkle', 'Wee Todger' and 'Pee Pee'.

## Morrissey – SEMI-SORRY

'My cup is only ever half-full, and it's half-day closing, on my half-term break in Hertfordshire,' laments the Manc genius and iconic Smiths frontman, only partly apologising for this collection of suitably laconic songs. Revel in the singalong sounds of 'Shrouded in Sadness', 'Buried in Badness', 'Gladiola Gladness' and 'Married to Madness'.

## Natalie Imbruglia – I'M LATE IN BULGARIA

Autobiographical and deeply sentimental offering from the doe-eyed Australian beauty about queuing to buy a pregnancy test in Sofia.

## Deacon Blue – UNCODEABLE

A welcome comeback from the Scottish pop-rockers with a collection of ceilidh dances, none of which you will understand. 'Boat to Stranraer', 'Schcudna Pudna in the Wee Dune Jimmy' and 'I Lost You in the Himiny-Hominy' are the only tracks that are vaguely decipherable.

## Britney Spears – PRESBYTERIANS

Newly dried out and looking for musical guidance, Britney turns to the Bible in the first of two simultaneous releases. Apparently, she's going to heaven and Kevin Federline is going to hell. Amen.

## Britney Spears – BRITNEY'S PEARS

Proving that it's not all about complicated word wizardry in Anagramland, the troubled Ms Spears-Federline-Other One gives us pop classics such as 'Jubblees', 'Fun Bags' and 'Hooters.' Not gratuitous at all then.

## Marvin Gaye – RE: MY VAGINA

Wonderful concept album in which Gaye's songs are reimagined as one long flirty intra-office email.

## Whitesnake – WAKE THE SIN

The challenge, it seems, with most David Coverdale productions is to see how many euphemisms for the male genitalia one can come up with during the course of a long player (oops, there's one already). Grab the Crass Thesaurus (ha, 'The Sore-Arse'!) then and listen out for the erotic sounds of 'Torpedo of Love', 'Loaded Rifle', ''Ere Jack, You're Late' and the ultra-subtle 'Ten Inches of Throbbing Love Muscle's Coming Your Way, Baby'. Who needs chocolates and roses when you've got the 'Snake around?

## Judas Priest – JUPITER'S SAD

Darkness abounds on this astronomically good CD
from the devilish Masters of the Occult. Watch out
for the hidden track at the end which when played
backwards spells out 'Murder the Badger' in Greek.
Expect an RSPCA inquiry at the Acropolis next year
following a spate of badger deaths and one beaver –
they're not big on zoology in Greece.

## Lily Allen – LLAINELLY

Stunning Welsh tribute album from the
extraordinarily talented Ms Allen. You try coming up
with something better with four Ls. Do I come to
where you work and tell you how to do your job?

## Muse – EMUS

Picking up the Floyd's 'animals' mantle, Devon's
finest sing about the second largest birds in the
world for forty-four quite long minutes. 'Flightless',
'Be Careful up There, Rod', and 'Why the Fuck
Does This Guy Have His Hand up My Arse?' are the
album's only high points.

## Guns 'n' Roses – GNUS 'N' 'ORSES

Convinced that Muse have found the Holy Grail of long-term commercial chart success, Axl and Slash deliver an East End knees-up, commemorating the great wildebeests and stallions of the world.

## The Eurythmics – MY HERETIC TUSH

Annie and Dave pay homage to Richard Dawkins' bottom.

## Foo Fighters – GHOST OF FIRE

Ten strikingly similar songs from the likeable American rockers, but who cares: the videos are super. The one for the title track, 'Ghost of Fire', filmed on Loch Ness at dusk whilst Urquhart Castle burns, cost more than Burkina Faso's national debt.

**Steve Fotherby** – THE VERY BEST OF . . .

Unknown New Zealand folk singer goes down the 'Very Best of' routine, attempting to convince the public that he's already very big down under (probably in Fiji, Tonga and the Cook Islands).

**Whitney Houston** – NON-WHITE YOUTHS

Enlisting the help of Puff Daddy, Puff Pastry and Puff the Magic Dragon, the revitalised Mrs Brown releases a heavyweight 'There's too much white in the stars 'n' stripes' Black Power album, although the contribution of the Magic Dragon is perhaps a little too fiery. Sorry.

**Michael Jackson** – HE CAN MOCK JAILS

Parental Advisory!

## Eric Clapton – NARCOLEPTIC

Old Slowhand releases a medley of guitar solos so
intricate they cause the brain to shut down in self-
defence.

## Posh Spice – CHOPS/PIES

In an attempt to prove that she's not really very thin,
Victoria lays down twelve tracks with that hugely
irritating electronic voice dub about fatty foods.
'Doughnut' will be the first single.

## **Gloria Estefan** – A LONGER FIESTA

Party time in Havana as the Miami Sound Machine
cruises downtown and plays the hypnotic 'Dr Beat'
for the entire Cuban holiday period. For the record,
'Dr Beat' was a worldwide hit in the eighties despite
this lyrical content:

Doctor, Doctor, won't you please help me, you gotta
    help me, you gotta help me.
If you got trouble, can't stop your feet, pay a little
    visit to Doctor Beat.
Doc, Doc, Doc, Doc, Doctor Beat
Doc, Doc, Doc, Doc, Doctor Beat
Doc, Doc, Doc, Doc, Doctor Beat
Doc, Doc, Doc, Doc, Doctor Beat.

Maybe it's deeper than I think.

## **Slipknot** – PINK SLOT

This is definitely not deeper than you think. The
masked rockers compose a paean to female
genitalia. We. Didn't. Need. This.

## Mike Oldfield – MIDDLE FOLKIE

Middle of the road. Folk Music. Music for Folk. With beards. 'Tubular Bells' may have stayed in the charts for 279 weeks, but this bollocks won't last 279 seconds on my iPod.

## Green Day – RENEGADY

Kids are good, adults are bad. Tommy goes to war, Tommy gets killed. Wear eyeliner. Blame the government.

## Cradle of Filth – THE FLORID CALF

Delightful set of tunes from the 'Filthers' that includes such pleasantries as 'Bleeding Mass of Gore', 'Putrid Stench of Wasted Entrails' and 'Aborting, Pollution, Destruction, Amen'. Bet they were much too old before a girl let them touch her boobies.

## Get the Sitars – GREATEST HITS

Finally the infamous 'Curry Chart' gets laid down on vinyl thanks to Bradford's finest, Get the Sitars. Features the magnificent single 'Things Can Only Get Butter Chicken'.

## Kanye West – SWEATY KEN

Cool Kanye adopts the concept of the Slim Shady persona and appears on his new release as Sweaty Ken. Reports that it is based on Ken Livingstone's apology for those naughty things he said to a journalist are unfounded.

## Lisa Scott-Lee – I LOST SALE, ETC.

Determined to keep the dream alive by any means whatsoever, the diminutive ex-Steps star (Lisa was in Steps, you know) manages to find time in between every single reality TV show to donate to the music industry the likes of 'Step Back to Happiness', 'The 39 Steps' and 'Steppy Steppy Step Step'. Before going solo, Lisa was in Steps. Along with the scraggly-headed H.

This is a fine reason for embracing the anagram album project – there would be no more H.

## **Stereophonics** – POSH ERECTIONS

Now revitalised after the sacking of the big hairy one on drums, Kelly and co. come at us hard and fast with an album jam-packed full of songs about upper-class boners. I personally love the two ballads, 'The Eton Rifle' and 'The Harrow Marrow'.

## **One Night Only** – LENGTHY ONION

Indie popsters celebrate large veg. 'Big Bean' and 'Enormous Turnip' are superb.

## **Miles Davis** – SADISM (LIVE)

The album title needs absolutely no explanation if you've ever been to a Miles Davis concert. This extraordinary noise, lasting a hellish sixty-four minutes, justifies fully the label of 'Jazz Is Shit'.

**Andrea Bocelli** – BALLADEER ICON

Doing exactly what it says on the tin, the iconic Italian sings ballads.

**Natasha Bedingfield** – THE BAND SANG, I FAILED

Doing exactly what it says on . . .

**Pussycat Dolls** – LADY'S COP SLUTS

Upping the ante somewhat after the cheeky goading of 'Don't Cha Wish Your Girlfriend Was Hot Like Me?', the saucy sextet's new album includes the singles 'Isn't It Interesting How My Mother Has Aged Better than Yours', 'Look at Your Frumpy Sister-in-Law' and 'Go on, Admit It, I Am Significantly More Attractive than Anyone You Have Ever Been Allowed to Touch, You Pathetic, Useless Virgin'.

**Katherine Jenkins** – HER KINKI NET JEANS

Phwoooaarrrr!

## Busta Rhymes – BUSTY HAREMS

Tip-top hip-hop from Old Busta with a lot of booty and babylons lurking around. Do your utmost to comprehend songs such as 'Bitchin' Wit Ya', 'Do It Dat Way', 'Actually Do It Dis Way' and 'Do It Eider Way, I Don't Give a Funk'.

## Fall Out Boy – FULLY TABOO

The most unlikely looking megastars of pop rock go dark and mysterious with their new release. 'Fully Taboo' uses the F word, the B word, the C word and the K word – whatever that is.

## Motorhead – DEATHROOM

Lemmy and the gang return with a somewhat disappointing array of songs that never quite match the awesome 'Ace of Spades'. Of the fourteen tracks, only 'King of Clubs', 'Two of Diamonds' and 'Five of Hearts' have any real depth.

## White Stripes – SWEETISH TRIP

Moroccan Dubies, Beijing Bonging, Cloudsurfing and Kaleidoscopic Ecstasy – it's all here. Welcome to Jack and Meg's magical journey.

## Westlife – I WET SELF

Refreshingly honest bedwetting collection of tracks from the loveable Irish boys, including a brilliant cover of Coldplay's 'Yellow'.

## Pigeon Detectives – GIVE TO CENTIPEDES

Band Aid, Children in Need, Red Nose Day and now this. Goodness gracious.

## Nelly Furtado – NOD TEARFULLY

Oh cheer up Nelly! What's the worst that could happen? Another album probably.

## **Meat Loaf** – A FAT MOLE

Just the three songs on this one, all with
extraordinarily long titles. Track 1, entitled 'If Loving
You Is So Very Wrong, I Don't Ever Wanna Feel Right
Again', starts slowly and builds to an anthemic chorus
with a female guest singer and weighs in at just under
eight and a half minutes. Track 2, which borders on
half an hour, 'I Cried Myself to Sleep Last Night, Yet
the Tear-Stained Pillows Are Still Here in the
Morning', again starts really slowly, but then
reassuringly builds to a big ending with contributing
vocals from an unknown female singer. The finale,
'I've Run a Marathon of Madness to Be Here Tonight,
But All You've Done Is Let Me Down Again, Which I
Don't Think Is Particularly Fair, Given the Troubles
I've Had with Public Transport This Evening, Honestly
the Buses Were Just Awful and Anyway, Do You Know
How Expensive It Is from Stoke?', has a running time
of just over four days, but does start slowly and finish
climactically with a cacophony of female singers with
great voices. The accompanying videos all take place
in the fog within a large, secluded manor house at
midnight. At some stage Meat will gaze into a mirror
and see a somewhat macabre reflection.

## Russell Watson – TENOR'S ALL WUSS

He is a bit, isn't he?

## Robert Plant – PORN BATTLER

Taking an admirable stance on the smutty world of online sex, the Planter pleads with his audience in 'Keeping the Keyboard Clean' and 'Stairway to Seven Years Inside'.

## Alicia Keys – A LAKE IS ICY

A Valentine's Day bestseller from the queen of truisms:
Baby
Baby Baby
Baby Don't Go
Baby Come Back
Baby Get Your Arse Back Here Now
Baby You're the One
Baby a Lake Is Icy (and You Are Really Nicey)
Baby Doll
Baby Food
Baby Gap
Nobody Puts Baby in the Corner
Baby Baby Baby

## Eva Cassidy – A DAY'S VICES

These include fly-tipping, stealing pens from W. H. Smith and football hooliganism. Who'd have thought she had it in her?

## Kings of Leon – FOOKING LENS

The hairy family has a spot of bother with the camera.

## Alesha Dixon – I HAD SEX ON AL

Al Gore? Al Green? Al Capone? Al Fayed? Al Jolson? Al Pacino? Al Murray? The Dancing Queen keeps us guessing.

## Amy MacDonald – MY ODD ANAL CAM

Utilising all the advantages of the internet, Amy produces a live-streaming follow-up to the excellent 'This Is the Life'. An eye-opener in the true sense of the word.

## The Cardigans – ARCADE NIGHTS

Nina Persson and friends dedicate this new offering
to the wild times they had recording their debut
album, evening after evening playing those Malmö
slot machines. It gets dark early in Sweden.

## Myleene Klass – SEEMLY ANKLES

The ivory-tinkling minx demonstrated all her
charms in the jungle – including those delicate,
slender, rose-scented feet. What I wouldn't give for a
touch of Klass . . . but unfortunately, new aggressive
anti-stalking legislation means I probably never will.

## Kate Nash – HE'S A TANK

Cockney-rhyming quirkiness from the cute and
chubby songstress. Opening track 'I Hid a Turd in
Your Trainer' sets the tone for the next nine
fetchingly juvenile numbers.

## James Blunt – NAME BJ SLUT

A whole album that centres on Hugh Grant's infamous misdemeanour, including the shockingly awful single, 'You Were Too Good for Him, Liz'.

## Luciano Pavarotti – TROPICANO VALUTAI

The big bearded fella pays tribute to his pop heroes Wham! The 'Nessun Dorma' mix of 'Young Guns (Having Some Fun)' is one of the most extraordinary things you will ever hear. And as for 'Ragazzi Cattivi' ('Bad Boys') . . .

## David Gray – I ADD GRAVY

David returns with another album for those who've had the capacity to feel real emotions pulled out of their nose with a coathanger. This time it's about how he improves every single thing he is ever given for dinner.

**Elbow** – BOWEL

Fairly unpleasant from start to finish, this one, and much longer than you realise, although the ballad 'Jobby' is OK.

**REM** – ERM?

Stipey goes all conceptual, chronicling the teenage years of a shy and insecure boy, easily embarrassed by everything. The NME will love it, without actually understanding a bloody thing that's going on.

**Sandi Thom** – AIDS MONTH

The vacuous queen of indistinct rebellion brings us this special EP released to coincide with an ill-advised season of programmes on *Men and Motors*.

## MacDonald Brothers – SCOTLAND BRAE D'MHOR

Gaelic gaiety from the two talentless turds who invaded our television screens for more weeks than I care to remember. This will be big in the Cairngorns and should stay there. For ever.

## Portishead – POT I SHARED

Beth Gibbons (no, that's not an anagram) lists all of the times she's shared her stash with her housemates, even though they never pay for anything and honestly it's not really on and why do people always feel they can take advantage of me, it's because I'm such a generous person isn't it, because I'm a Buddhist. Has anyone got any biscuits?

## Al Green – GENERAL

The man with the voice of honey sings proudly about his own member. Apparently it's more of a lance corporal.

## Chas and Dave – CAN DAD SHAVE?

Just when you thought it was safe to go into HMV, the purveyors of 'Rabbit', 'Gertcha' and 'Snooker Loopy' return with 'Can Dad Shave?' Expect lines such as 'My dad Mick, he's got a Bic, whoops cor blimey, there's a little nick'. And that's the good stuff. Remarkably, there is in existence an album entitled *The Best of Chas and Dave*. It's all relative I suppose.

## Foster and Allen – FORESTLAND LANE

Bordering on excruciating, the ageing nasal duo snort their way through an hour of songs about the pretty girl from the farm over the road – no chance, lads, no chance.

## Neil Diamond – I MIND NO LEAD

Controversial effort from the New Yorker, encouraging us all to revert to leaded petrol. He'll be asking us all to listen to 'Sweet Caroline' again next.

## Iron Maiden – DEMON IN AIR

Frontman Bruce Dickinson is a qualified pilot. Now, if he could just learn to sing . . .

## Ms Katie Price – I'M PRICK TEASE

Indeed.

## Peter Andre – A PRETENDER

Indeed.

## Rick Astley – REAL STICKY

The Prince of Big Hair sings about the state of his pants after a difficult session with Pete Waterman.

## The Notorious BIG – SHOOTING OUR BETI

A surprisingly gentle collection of tunes here from
Notorious, released as a tribute to his cousin Beti,
who was the forty-third member of his family to be
gunned down in gangland revenge killings.
Rumours are he watched a lot of *Coronation Street*
while writing the album.

## Gary Glitter – GIRLY TARGET

Who says anagrams can't be edgy?

## Michael Bolton – A MOONLIT BELCH

The mega-mullet man explains how love got away
from him one night when he went to sing in his
fiancée's ear and burped. 'It happened so quick,
just me, the moonlight and a mouthful of sick.'

## Stevie Wonder – SEVERED IN TWO

A sad autobiographical CD that explains what happened the first time Stevie tried to cut his own toenails.

## The Rolling Stones – LINGERS THEN LOOTS

Mick and the crew highlight the rise in car crime with an album that centres on the epic 'Hey You, Get off of My Clio'.

## The Doors – SO RED HOT

'Come On Baby, Light My Fire' – that's all, I'm afraid.

## Curtis Mayfield – RIDICULES MY FAT

An insecure offering from the king of funky bass and wah-wah, containing tracks such as 'Where Have All the Pies Gone?' and 'When a Man Cannot See His Own Balls (Is He Really Even a Man?)'.

## Tommy Lee – MY OMELET

The tattooed maestro sings about finding eggs, butter and milk in his cupboard. Although what he does with them is a different thing entirely. The instrumental 'Batter' is apparently a tribute to the great cook Fanny.

## Smokey Robinson – MY KNOB'S EROSION

A desperately sad double album. The closing number, 'Flaky', is truly touching.

## Marilyn Manson – ONLY MAN IN MARS

The scariest man in rock (i.e. school nerd) puts on a bit of make-up and pretends to be David Bowie. Oooooooooooh!

## Spandau Ballet – LAUDABLE PANTS?

Tony and the troops wonder whether they really did look fucking stupid in those huge black trousers and baggy white shirts. This is a shocking collection of New Romantic reworkings that includes Simon and Garfunkel's 'The Boxer Shorts', the Village People's 'YMCA Fronts' and the Jam's 'Going Underpants'.

## Sir Bob Geldof – BIDS FOR GLOBE

Give us yer fucking money!

# Desert Island Discs Anagram Special

QUEEN – 'Bohemian Shopyard'

BONNIE TYLER – 'Total Eclipse of the Earth'

ROLF HARRIS – 'Two Little Yobs'

EURYTHMICS – 'Sweet Dreams Are Made of Shit'

SQUEEZE – 'Annie Get Your Gnu'

ROBBIE WILLIAMS – 'Let Me Enter You, Tina'

ELTON JOHN – 'Snog for Guy'/'I Guess That's
   Why They Calls it the Lube'

STEVIE WONDER – 'I Just Called to Say "You Olive"'

# FOOTBALL

Footballers are great for anagrams; indeed, my whole fantasy football team is often based entirely on who has a ridiculous name. Never put **David O'Leary** in charge of your team, by the way. He's one to *Avoid Dearly,* and **Milan Baros** *Is Abnormal.* Maybe that's why O'Leary signed him for Villa. And we all know **Big Ron Atkinson** *Is Ignorant Knob.*

How wrong Brian Barwick was, believing that **Steve McClaren** was the *Cleverest Man(c)* for the England job before our abject failure to qualify for Euro 2008. And as for the previous national team manager, a philandering Scandinavian who picked a schoolboy to sit on the bench for the entire duration of the world's biggest tournament: **Sven-Goran Eriksson** clearly never heeded the advice of FA headquarters when they suggested to him, '*Never Risk a Snog, Son.*'

Manchester United's **Gary Neville** is, revealingly, *Revealingly.* No really, it is revealingly. Worryingly, rather than revealingly, Gary Neville's father is called Neville. *Neville Neville.* An anagram without moving any letters around. How fantastic is that? **Eric Cantona** claimed, '*I Cannot Care,*' although in fairness he said an awful lot of other nonsense to do with sardines and trawlers, so that's not altogether conclusive. Other soccer delights include **Chris Sutton** or *Ostrich Nuts* as he was for me, *Dead Muffin* (**Damien Duff**) and *Saggy Ring* (**Ryan Giggs**). The award for the most prophetic anagram goes to **Diego Forlan** – *Fired No Goal.*

I was particularly glad when ex-Bayern Munich and France full back Bixente Lizarazu retired. That's not a name, that's someone tripping over a Scrabble board.

See if you can get these football-related anagrams.

*Answers at the back.*

# The Alternative England

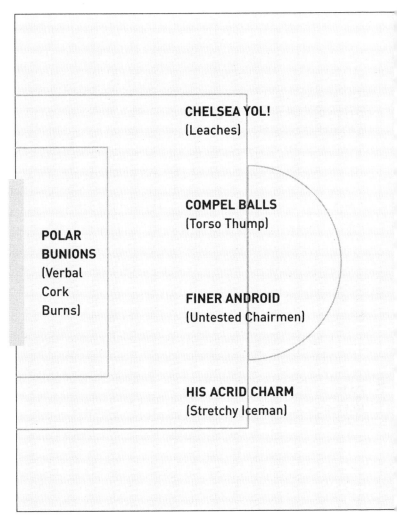

CHELSEA YOL!
(Leaches)

COMPEL BALLS
(Torso Thump)

POLAR
BUNIONS
(Verbal
Cork
Burns)

FINER ANDROID
(Untested Chairmen)

HIS ACRID CHARM
(Stretchy Iceman)

*Butt Tissues:*
**This Purplish-Whaling** (Leaches)
**Boner Fest** (Untested Chairmen)

# Anagram Football XI

**as of the start of the 2008/2009 season**

**WONDERING TWATS**
(Dig Bum Holders)

**PARKLAND FARM**
(Leaches)

**I LEACH WOMEN**
(Lettuces and Wine)

**AVENGE WARHORSE**
(Untested Chairmen)

**CROTCH PUREE**
(Torso Thump)

**DANGER REVERTS**
(Oil Plover)

**Grab Her Tray** (Vital Loans)
**He's Only A Guy** (Vital Loans)
**Earn New Yoyo** (Untested Chairmen)

# PREMIERSHIP BLEAT 2007/2008

| Pos | Team |
| --- | --- |
| 1 | Untested Chairmen |
| 2 | Leaches |
| 3 | Analers |
| 4 | Oil Plover |
| 5 | Ten Over |
| 6 | Vital Loans |
| 7 | Verbal Cork Burns |
| 8 | Torso Thump |
| 9 | Stretchy Iceman |
| 10 | Team with Nudes |
| 11 | The Photo Tantrums |
| 12 | Lettuces and Wine |
| 13 | Dig Bum Holders |
| 14 | Waiting Chalet |
| 15 | Nun Ladders |
| 16 | Newborn Leotards |
| 17 | Ham Flu |
| 18 | Nag Ride |
| 19 | Bathing Mimicry |
| 20 | Body Century |

By the way, these are my favourite continental clubs. See if you can get them.

**Spain:** Real Bacon
**Italy:** Mini Rental
**Germany:** Bun Machinery
**Holland:** Potter's Art Drama
**France:** It Inspires Anagram
**Portugal:** Bristling Spoon
**Belgium:** Bugger

| Manager | Ground |
|---|---|
| I Flex Señora's Rug | Dr Afford Lot |
| Vagrant Ram | For Drab Midgets |
| Renew Enrages | Sited Amateurism |
| Tzarina Beef | Flea Din |
| My Sad Video | Spooking Road |
| I'm Not a Niller | Krap Villa |
| He Shag Mr UK | Weak Droop |
| Drank Happy Err | Rank Top Fart |
| Sneaks in Governors | Fat Synthetic Sodium Cream |
| I Can Really Bush | Kaput Porn |
| Majored Anus | There with Anal |
| KK – Naïve Gene | Spark Jetsam |
| Treat to Huge Shag | Diseased Triumvir |
| Beever Cuts | Just Bid Jam |
| Keno Year | Dismal Outfight |
| Gay Mongers | Ask Our Bedtime |
| Horny Goods | Vacant Cortege |
| Sell Covet Pep | Just Kiddie Mamas |
| Hi, Call Me Sex | Wants Reds! |
| We All Julep | Kid Rapper |

# POLITICS

The right to mock the great and good using anagrams was protected in English law when King John sealed **Magna Carta** (*Anagram Act*) in 1215.

Ever since then, people have had great fun mixing up the letters of famous people's names, and politicians are no exception. Some may argue that Mr Tony Blair was mixed up anyway, but a quick anagram check in 1997 would have revealed that his name was already shouting *I'm Tory Plan B.*

Equally pertinent is the briefly well-known Virginia Bottomley – *I'm an Evil Tory Bigot.* It is up there with the very best anagrams of all time.

Here is my top ten from the world of politics:

## Osama bin Laden
### – Bad Man Is Alone

## Saddam Hussein
### – I Had US Madness

George Bush
- He Bugs Gore

United States of America
- Deem It as an Utter Fiasco

Margaret Thatcher
- That Great Charmer

Nancy Reagan
- An Ace Granny

Lee Harvey Oswald
- Revealed Who Slay

Neil Kinnock
- I Knock Lenin

David Cameron
- A Divorced Man

Monica Lewinsky
- A Lick Wins Money

# REAL
# PEOPLE

Some people have a name that is an anagram of someone else's. Alice, for instance, uses the same letters as Celia. *Celia in Wonderland* would never have worked though, and wearing a celia band on your head would be plain stupid. On the boys' side, there is an interchanging between Noel and Leon. Leon Edmonds? Noel Trotsky? A Christmas carol that begins 'The first Leon'? Some things just shouldn't be swapped, although I do like the idea of Leon Edmonds hosting a new show called *Lead or No Lead*, based on Russian roulette, with contestants deciding whether or not there is a bullet in the gun before pulling the trigger. The much-loved phrase 'I think there's another round in there' would certainly take on a whole new meaning.

Oh, and don't get me started on the Princess-Diana-and-Nadia-from-*Big Brother* conspiracy theories!

There are a few incredibly lucky people in the world, who have a Christian name that is an anagram of their surname. Actor Robert Trebor, for example, and ex-cricketer Brian Brain both possess this remarkable attribute. So I really hope the following people exist somewhere in the world. If you know of them, write to me and I'll include them in my next book. Probably.

## Eric Rice – Most likely an author

## Lionel O'Neill – Priest

**Cyril Lyric** – Composer

**Daniel Denial** – Conman

**Darren Errand** – Office junior

**Amber Bream** – Actress

**Basil Bails** – May actually have played cricket with Brian Brain

**Douglas USA Gold** – Pretentious American bastard who plans to win every single medal at the London Olympics in 2012

**Karl Lark** – Comedian

**Ivan Vain** – Ballet dancer

**Nancy Canny** – Code-breaker

**Kristina Airstink** – Environmental hygienist

**Lucas Claus** – Santa's son

**Glenda Dangle** – Porn star

**Alan Anal** – Gay porn star

**Ingrid Riding** – Sloane Ranger

**Lance Clean** – Willy washer

**Kay Yak** – Canoeist

**Olga Goal** – Gymnast

**Orlando Ronaldo** – Very handsome and talented actor/footballer

**Otto Toot** – Politician

**Pam Map** – Cartographer

**Lydia Daily** – Agony aunt – and indeed, good advice that; I certainly try to Lydia Daily

**Stephanie Penis-Hate** – Woman's Libber

**Miles Limes** – Art critic

**Gary Argy** – Hooligan

**Levi Evil** – Murderer

**Andrew Wander** – Explorer

**Reginald Il Grande** – Chairman of the Pompous Old Gits Club

**Callum Macull** – Hebridean seal-basher

**Adolf Faldo** – Nazi golfer

**Craig Cigar** – Editor

**Liam Mail** – Postman

**Greta Grate** – Cook

**Pat Tap** – Plumber

**Lois Soil** – Gardener

**Vera Rave** – Dancer

**Winifred Windfire** – Farter

# DR
# ANAGRAM
# #1

PATIENT: Good morning, Dr Anagram.

DOCTOR: Good morning, how can I help you today?

PATIENT: It's my ears, Doctor.

DOCTOR: Your arse, eh?

PATIENT: Er ... yes, my ears, they're a bit blocked.

DOCTOR: Ah, constipation, very nasty.

PATIENT: Well yes it is, but my ears ...

DOCTOR: Tell me, do you get the occasional ringing sound in your arse?

PATIENT: Um, no, not really.

DOCTOR: Any wax up there?

PATIENT: I think there might be, yes.

DOCTOR: Could be a case of Irritable Elbow Syndrome. Tell you what, take these, and come back and see me in two weeks.

# GEOGRAPHY

# Capital Cities

Japan and Indonesia have excellent credentials when it comes to anagram notoriety. Both countries had anagrammatised their capitals into new ones. The Indonesians swapped Kartasura for Surakarta, whilst Japan's former capital was Kyoto – then they moved it to Tokyo of course.

So this got me thinking.

Here are my top twenty new capitals of the world in descending order:

| Country | Old Name | New Name |
| --- | --- | --- |
| 20) Denmark | Copenhagen | Open Change |
| 19) Mauritius | Port Louis | Our Pistol |
| 18) New Zealand | Wellington | Lentil Gown |
| 17) Argentina | Buenos Aires | Serious Bean |
| 16) Serbia | Belgrade | Bread Leg |

| 15) Chile | Santiago | A Goat Sin |
| 14) Jamaica | Kingston | Stink Nog |
| 13) Belgium | Brussels | Rubs Less |
| 12) USA | Washington DC | Watchdogs Inn |
| 11) Brazil | Brasilia | Sir Labia |
| 10) Romania | Bucharest | Bra Chutes |
| 9) Panama | Panama City | Captain Yam |
| 8) Norway | Oslo | Loos |
| 7) Singapore | Singapore | Opera Sing |
| 6) Mongolia | Ulan Bator | Anal Turbo |
| 5) Trinidad & Tobago | Port of Spain | Parsnip Foot |
| 4) Pakistan | Islamabad | Bad Salami |
| 3) Scotland | Edinburgh | Inbred Hug |
| 2) Holland | Amsterdam | Edam Trams |

But Haiti's Port-au-Prince wins the Award for Best Choice, as the Haitians could happily rename their capital one of the following.

| Apricot Prune | Pin-up Creator | Panic Trouper |
| Toucan Ripper | Crap Eruption | Terrapin Coup |
| Apron Picture | Citron Pauper | Porcupine Art |

# Top Ten Countries

1)     Anti Anger

2)     Bag Handles

3)     Safari Touch

4)     Moon Race

5)     Spa Region

6)     Sad All Over

7)     Game Habit

8)     Inebriated Amateurs

9)     Diva's Helmet

10)    Erotic Video                      *Answers at the back.*

# NUL POINTS

**The Eurovision Song Contest** is, of course, where the *Grooviest Tune is Not Chosen*

Hence why artists like Lordi win.

Or maybe it is because of the *Not-so-secret In-house Voting*.

But one thing's for sure, with all the pre-qualifying and semi-finals now, *The Convention's Got Serious*. Actually these anagrams are more interesting than the show itself. Although *Terry Wonga* is good.

Incidentally Jemini (last in 2003) is *not* an anagram of 'hopeless wankers'.

*Fucks Bizz* deserve a mention. *Johnny Along* probably doesn't. *Sandie Wash* probably didn't.

Euro legends *Baba* should still be going, I reckon. Much better use of Benny, Agnetha, Björn and Anni-Frid.

By the way, what would have happened if the four members of Abba had been called Frederik, Ulrika, Conrad and Kristina?

*Fuck the Musical*, I guess.

# Films

**Hollywood** is the perfect place for jumbled words. The home of the film industry presents us with its own anagram movies, such as *Lowly Hood*, a hard-hitting, brutal account of life as part of a midget gang in the suburbs of Los Angeles, and *Hold Wooly*, a kind of *Free Willy* for the shepherding community. The porn industry would not be backward in coming forward either with its own ninety-minute spanking classic, *Oh Ow Dolly*, and don't forget the Bollywood contribution, *Bloody Owl*, a low-budget offering, which follows the frustrated dancing of an angry farmer who keeps finding shit in his barn.

Here's a comprehensive list of movies engineered from the very letters of their stars' names. So look out for these anagram blockbusters coming to a cinema screen near you very soon.

## BIG LEMONS

**Mel Gibson** is an Australian simpleton who makes his living selling large pieces of fruit from the family greengrocers on the outskirts of Hobart. He absolutely does not say anything anti-Semitic. At any point.

## GERMANY

**Meg Ryan** stars in this modern-day portrayal of the real Fatherland. Outstanding moments include a lot of blokes in coloured jackets waxing lyrical about Nena's '99 Red Balloons' and Meg Ryan scoring the winner in a penalty shoot-out against England.

## IN MOCK DENIAL

Tense courtroom drama starring **Nicole Kidman** as a key witness to a murder who continues to deny her involvement while challenging the legal establishment. Probably written by John Grisham.

## A LARDY MONG

**Gary Oldman** is magnificent in this biographical epic documenting the life and times of Rik Waller. In true 'method' style, to get ready for playing the lead Gary ate pies.

## TOM AND TAM

Handsome **Matt Damon** plays both Scottish twins in a delightful tale of a pair of Hebridean islanders wanting to hit the big time. They make it as far as Pitlochry.

## A JOCK'S LOCH INN

**Jack Nicholson** plays a mad Glaswegian landlord who invites strangers for after-hours drinking. He takes all the women roughly over the kitchen table and kills all the men with an axe. He then gets sent to a mental institution where they cut his brain out. Who said anything about typecasting?

## DOCILE OR PARANOID

**Leonardo DiCaprio** awakes from a coma in a Los Angeles hospital and in a semi-conscious haze believes he is under threat from every organisation in the world. Spend the next two and a half hours watching young Leo run from the FBI, the CIA, the KGB, MI5, MFI, B&Q, the BBC, the TUC, the RUC, the YMCA and the DISCO. Gene Hackman wins the inevitable Best Supporting Actor Oscar for his part as Harry Jamieson, head of the CIA. Sadly H from Steps wins bugger all for his role as head of DISCO.

## IN MY NORMA ROLE

**Marilyn Monroe** relates an autobiographical and heart-rending account of the first time she had posthumously to sit through 'Candle in the Wind'.

## REFUELS IN THE DARK

**Kiefer Sutherland** runs out of petrol on a lonely road at midnight in redneck country. When the pump attendant informs him that he sure has a pretty mouth, Kiefer has twenty-four hours to drive pointlessly around, talking into a mobile phone.

## OVEN STRICKEN

**Kevin Costner** has made a lot of shit over the years and this may well top the lot, as he takes care of an Aga left out in the rain at the local tip. Worryingly, it is still better than *Waterworld*.

## WHY RISK ANAL?

Double Oscar winner **Hilary Swank** aims to make it a hat-trick of Academy Awards in this Marquis de Sade-type tale of the unexpected.

## ALL SUCK ON BRAD

**Sandra Bullock** joins Angelina Jolie and Jennifer Aniston in a story of lust and betrayal and a bit more lust. The climax, where the hat-trick of heroines work on Brad's *spine* all at the same time, will have you reaching for the pause button with monotonous regularity.

## WINKLE TASTE
## *(ALL SUCK ON BRAD II)*

**Kate Winslet** joins Sandra Bullock, Angelina Jolie and Jennifer Aniston in the erotic sequel, where the four protagonists all enjoy Brad's *cheekbones*.

## REVENGE IS OUR WAY

**Sigourney Weaver** gets on a spaceship and heads off to the planet Voldark to kill a load of little green-headed bastards which she missed the last time. Either that, or she marries a gorilla to get back at her cheating husband.

## SACRED ALIEN

**Claire Danes** signs up with a cult in downtown Doncaster who worship the 'God of Visitation', an alien vision that appears on Thursdays after bingo.

## FARCICAL TALK HOST

The actress with the largest nostrils in the universe, **Calista Flockhart**, plays a goofy presenter who continually fucks things up.

## BIG MELONS

**Mel Gibson** teams up with Dolly Parton, Jordan and that frightening Leah from *Big Brother* in a hilarious 'Carry On'-type comedy with bosom gags galore. A must for Benny Hill fans. Still no mention of the Old Testament.

## OLD WEST ACTION

**Clint Eastwood** rides a horse, wears a hat, smokes cigars, kills Mexicans and shags the barkeeper's daughter. A cult classic.

## 'SILICONES' ARE VITAL

Young rookie cop **Alicia Silverstone** exposes the shady side of the increasingly persuasive breast augmentation market. Features strong language from the start, scenes of a graphic nature and some really big knockers.

## ORWELL'S CURSE

The much-anticipated follow-up to the brilliant *1984* and *Animal Farm* sees **Russell Crowe** trying to save the world from a pig and a horse in the year 4981.

## GENUINE CLASS

Ealing comedy with **Alec Guinness**. Dull as fuck.

## I DO ME MORE

Following the subtle brilliance of *Striptease*, **Demi Moore** goes on another journey of self-exploration. Look out for cameo appearances from David Ginola and Axl Rose.

## SHORTCAKE HUNT

**Ashton Kutcher** tracks down a long-lost biscuit. Crumbs!

## ONE WILD HAG

**Goldie Hawn** is a bedraggled old hoofer – actually I'll stop there.

## CARAMEL CENTRE

**Carmen Electra** and a box of liquidy truffles. 'Nuff said.

## CANCEL THAT BET

A remake of the classic Marx Brothers farce, starring **Cate Blanchett**, in which she spends the whole film trying to stop a bet that she placed on Theo Walcott ever playing for England.

## CRIED AMAZON

**Cameron Diaz** stars in this heady drama set in deepest Brazil. The earth is dying, the rainforests are on fire and the banks of the world's greatest river are breaking. All of this ain't great, but Cameron's arse looks champion.

## PHANTOM MEMOS

**Emma Thompson** uncovers a load of ghostly Post-It notes in a really posh film that will most likely be a remake of a Shakespeare play. For the first time in cinema history, Kenneth Branagh doesn't appear with her.

## VAGINA SEED

**Geena Davis** stars in this beautiful, superbly moving account of the miracle of childbirth. Davis is outstanding as the single mother who is desperate to have a baby and gives up everything to pursue her dream. The music score is full of tear-jerking emotive ballads, the cinematography is groundbreaking and Geena's muff is excellent.

## INSANE MOLE

**Liam Neeson** is a mad undercover agent who uses all the tricks of the trade to get the job done: crosses, double crosses, counter-crosses as well as noughts and crosses. After an hour, you'll be so farting confused, you'll wish you'd gone to see *A Lardy Mong*.

## IRISH LEAFS

Ravishing redhead **Isla Fisher** plays a ravishing redhead from Dun Laoghaire. Autumnal settings and a lot of fiddly-dee – no doubt Daniel Day-Lewis will turn up, act the bastard and smack our flaxen heroine around a bit.

## ALL CHARM IS LEGAL HERE

More bizarre Buffyness with **Sarah Michelle Gellar**, and the good news is that after ten minutes, she snogs one of her fellow actresses like she did in *Cruel Intentions*. You can leave then.

## MAUVE RAINS

**Mena Suvari** and Prince team up for the sequel to his 1980s classic *Purple Rain*. There are a few more drops this time and they're a wee bit darker. The climax sees the pair huddled up under the cliffs, praying for the storm to pass with the epic Prince soundtrack 'When Coves Dry' playing in the distance.

## ACTUAL JOHNNIES

**Anjelica Huston** plays a high-class call girl who insists on using genuine condoms only – as opposed to cling film.

## I'LL CURB WISE

**Bruce Willis** plays Kevin Keegan in this true story of life at St James' Park. Willis's wig is super and Paul Danan as Dennis Wise is worryingly believable.

## I DUPE MY HERD

**Eddie Murphy** stars as a shepherd who constantly takes the rise out of his sheep.

## HOODLESS BIKER

With **Brooke Shields**. Try and spend an hour and a half without mentioning how different Ms Shields looks from the way she did in *Blue Lagoon*, where she starred alongside that skinny chisel. As a crazed member of a gang of Hell's Angels, Brooke is totally believable as she murders her way across most of Peru. The theme tune, 'The Screamer from Lima', is awesome.

## OBSCENELY WOKEN

Songstress **Beyoncé Knowles** plays a young American singer who awakes from a nightmare in which her original band reforms, so that once more she has to appear on stage with the ugly one.

## DYNATROLLOP

**Dolly Parton** is at her most inspiring best as the outlandish boss of an all-female plumbing company. Crude tool-type jokes aplenty from start to finish and more innuendos than you can shake a fish at.

## RAMPANT TOENAIL

Foot fetishism abounds as seedy nightclub owner **Natalie Portman** has each and every pinkie licked by bad boys Ice T, Ice Cream and Ice Cube. The erotic climax where Naughty Nat has her big toe sucked by Ice Wallow will live long in your memory.

## MARTIN'S UNCLE

Remarkable adaptation of the very popular *Doc Martin* television series featuring **Martin Clunes**. In this gripping feature-length film about everyday life in a sleepy Cornish village, the local community is stunned when Martin receives a visit from a relative. Tense and unpredictable, the scene where the two relations attend the local St Minver summer fête is unmissable.

## POOR 'N' TWEE HEIRESS

The ever-so-cutesy **Reese Witherspoon** plays a sweet orphan who suddenly finds herself in line to inherit a fortune, having been adopted by a mad old buffoon (Sir Bobby Robson). A host of jealous sisters and would-be suitors place this right up there with *Legally Blonde* and *Little Nicky* in the realms of bollocks cinema.

## PETER IS SO NOWHERE

Follow-up to *Poor 'n' Twee Heiress*. Follows the tribulations of **Reese Witherspoon** as she tries to locate Peter, the man she married who then buggered off with all her cash. Reese screams a lot and wears pink – like that improves the movie.

## WHITE ROSE REOPENS

**Reese Witherspoon** never did find Peter, but not to worry; she relocates to Huddersfield and finds love rekindled in the county of Yorkshire with local butcher Rodney Rowebottom.

## WHEN I SEE TROOPERS

Sadly for Rod, he's dropped like one of his own sausages when **Reese Witherspoon** bumps into some American paras on manoeuvres in Rotherham. Still screaming, still pink.

## ICE TUMORS

**Tom Cruise** plays a cheeky charmer who smiles at women, who then pull their pants down. Meanwhile Cruise has to decode a scary virus that is implanting freezing cold chunks into the brains of some of the world's political leaders. Just in time, our dashing hero invents a neurological blowtorch that slowly melts the ice away and stops it from accessing the brain, or something. Hilary Clinton, played by Sharon Stone, is so impressed she pulls her pants down. Bill Clinton, played by Sharon Osborne, joins in.

## HE ATE KINKY GIRL

**Keira Knightley** dresses up in a scarlet-and-black basque and demands to be devoured. (Presumably she's the starter.)

## AUTUMN HARM

**Uma Thurman** does her own stunts in this hard-hitting action film, including slipping on wet leaves and getting bonfire smoke in her eyes. The scene where she puts the tortoise into hibernation is heartbreaking. Didn't do very well in the US because no one there knows what autumn is.

## FINDS A HORROR

**Harrison Ford** discovers a VHS copy of his own *Random Hearts* in the loft.

## COLEEN: HER PSALM

Once known as The Body and now pretty much The Nobody, **Elle MacPherson** plays Mrs Wayne Rooney in this charming dramatisation of Wozza and Coleen on their big day. Rumours are that filming was disrupted for three months while part of the crew worked on *Shrek 4*.

## NAZI COMRADE

**Cameron Diaz** stars as Yelena Schweinsteiger, a mightily confused spy who knows not her arse from her elbow. Or indeed her ears from her bowel.

## CHARITABLE SIN

Mad bastard **Christian Bale** lures vulnerable women-in-need back to his fancy New York apartment, gives them a glass of wine and a few honey-roasted nuts and then cuts their heads off. Who needs seduction techniques when you've got a big chainsaw in your larder?

## LET'S BERLIN

Fantastic follow-up to *Meet the Fockers*. **Ben Stiller** takes his family to Germany on vacation, where they encounter the Kuntz from Cologne. The good news is we only have to wait eighteen minutes before the highly predictable, yet still incredibly funny line, 'I don't think I'm gonna like those Kuntz.'

## DIES NOW

With *Eastenders'* **Sid Owen**. Keep your fingers crossed.

## MY PALE PARTS

Ricky's other half **Patsy Palmer** plays a freckly ginger girl with very white skin. Tough one that.

## TACKLER PAUL

**Petula Clark** was the somewhat surprising choice to play soccer supremo Paul Gascoigne, but she gives a whole-hearted performance as Gazza in this realistic portrayal of the England legend, whose career never recovered from the lunging challenge on Forest's Gary Charles (played by Leona Lewis) in the 1991 FA Cup Final. Petula's relationship with Jimmy 'Five Bellies' (played by Charlotte Church) is beautiful.

## SLID CARROT

**Traci Lords** gives all vegetarians nightmares for a year.

## I CANNOT LET HER SLIDE

*Desperate Housewives* star **Nicollette Sheridan** features in the brilliant sequel to *Slid Carrot,* in which she spends the whole film trying to wean Traci off the carrot sliding.

## PORK MESS

Gangland legend **Ross Kemp** laments his broken sausage.

## ANORAKS IN TOWN

**Rowan Atkinson** is the chairman of a trainspotting association visiting Burnley for their annual conference. Expect Atkinson to pull his hilarious Mr Bean gurning face on at least 138 different occasions.

## I RUB MY GOATEE

High-school nerd **Tobey Maguire** believes absolutely nothing in this charming American rom-com. He spends the whole film stroking his stubble and saying, 'Chinny reckon.' Maguire is currently working on the sequel, entitled *Mmm beard*.

## DREAM SANDAL

**Adam Sandler** plays a habitual somnambulist who one night finds an espadrille that transports him back to Jerusalem. He is soon healing the sick with the use of Nurofen and feeding lots of people with Mother's Pride and fish fingers. It's hysterical if you enjoyed *The Nutty Professor*, *Porkies* and *Police Academy 19*.

## COCAINE SLAG

A brave piece of casting; **Nicolas Cage** appears in his four-hundred-and-third film of the year in this sensitive biopic of Courtney Love.

## CELIBATE THRUSH

A modern-day Liverpudlian take on the Virgin Mary story starring **Elisha Cuthbert** as Pinot G, a Scouse schoolgirl who tries in vain to explain her predicament. Warning: contains scenes of a pessary nature.

## ONLY CHITS AND HURLS

**Nicholas Lyndhurst** struggles to rid himself of the Rodney Trotter tag in this clumsy comedy about a tall, thin man from Peckham who encounters some bills and a few things that have been thrown at him.

## HE CAN BREATHE NORMAL

English rose **Helena Bonham Carter** faces a race against time to find a ventolin inhaler for her wheezing husband (played by Antony Worrall Thompson). Mercifully, after an hour and twenty minutes of gasping noises and extremely heavy panting – and that's just Helena – she finds the little blue puffer, along with the remote control, the car keys and two triple A batteries.

## A LIMBLESS TIGER

Best known for her role as Laura Ingalls in *Little House on the Prairie*, **Melissa Gilbert** once more tugs her audience's heartstrings in this true story of Simon, a tiger born with no arms or legs who can only move by dragging himself about with a specially adapted Velcro tongue. It's like *Born Free*, but with no action.

## A CRIMSON BATH

Based on the best-selling horror novel by Stephen King, **Mischa Barton** lies in a deep tub with a lot of bubbles and a luxury loofah. Then the obligatory nutter arrives and discolours all the nice white lather.

## ANOTHER'S SON

**Sharon Stone** adopts a young boy orphaned after his whole family takes part in a disappointing bungee jump. Steve Martin plays Stone's boyfriend who offers the consoling line, 'Don't worry son, you'll bounce back.'

## IN THE TEENY PARADE

Everyone's favourite cheerleader **Hayden Panettiere** stars in this clever spin-off from the smash-hit series *Heroes*. She plays – wait for it – a cute cheerleader who becomes prom queen. Well I never. Go Hayden.

## IN EMAIL CACHE

There are no secrets in your Outlook Express. **Michael Caine**, address-book contacts and cookies. Will join *Zulu* and *Escape to Victory* on the list of Caine's most extraordinary films.

## MEDIA FELLOW

**Willem Dafoe** plays Max Clifford in this raw and explicit study of the UK press. Sadly, Clifford dies at the end when in an attempt to take credit for the sun rising he is stoned to death.

## I. RIISE lbw LAMB 0

**Robbie Williams** makes a stunning big-screen debut as cricketer Henry Lamb (son of ex-England international Allan). The title of the movie is taken from the climatic scene at Lord's where young Henry grabs his first ever test wicket, that of opener Ian Riise (son of hapless ex-Liverpool footballer John-Arne). The Norwegian lad is trapped in front by one that nips back off the seam for a duck. What do you mean, contrived? Took me hours this one.

## NO DANISH ALLY

Little **Lindsay Lohan** wakes up in a bed-and-breakfast on the outskirts of Aarhus. Lost and alone, she gets told to piss off by the whole of Denmark.

## MY HOT OLD TITAN

In an attempt to minimise its carbon footprint, MI6 is forced to make James Bond car-share a beat-up Nissan truck instead of his normal Aston Martin while on his latest US mission. This doesn't stop **Timothy Dalton** from having his merry way with a load of ultra-fit totty in suitably exotic locations, although he is careful to offset any emissions.

## DINKIER BRA KEN?

*Coronation Street*'s **Anne Kirkbride** questions whether her old flame would prefer a little lacy number. The film? Imagine an episode of *Corrie* and multiply it by three.

## NAIL CAPO

Godfather **Al Pacino** instructs his nastiest hitmen to track down the leader of a rival gang. Brutal violence and strong sexual content. These days that's a PG.

## A HI LOW MIRACLE

Known for his near fifty-year portrayal of **Ken Barlow** (*Lob Wanker*), **William Roache** plays a contestant on Bruce's *Play Your Cards Right* who accurately predicts the turn of every card to win a washing machine, some cut glass and a day at a health spa.

## MANDELA PERSONA

A most unusual choice to play the black anti-apartheid activist, but buxom blonde *Baywatch* queen **Pamela Anderson** pulls it off in some style. But then again she always does.

## FINE IN TORN JEANS

**Jennifer Aniston** – fine in anything, to be fair.

## JOHN ROTTEN'S CLASS 'A'

**Scarlett Johansson** is magnificent as Nancy Spungen in this brash punk rock chronology. Jonatan Johansson, the curly-haired ex-Charlton centre forward, is less good as Sid Vicious, however.

# TELEVISION

Of course we all know that *TV is one lie* but we still can't get enough of it.

I particularly like watching *A Question of Sport*. So much so, I think that they should do some spin-offs. A motor-racing special would be cool, entitled *A Question of Prost*. Or if the captains were really grumpy, we could have *A Question of Strop*. But surely the most interesting would be *A Question of Ports*: half an hour of *Arse Burke* asking the two teams various posers about Folkestone, Le Havre, Zeebrugge and Ostend.

My other favourite show is *Dragons' Den*, and I love the idea of the panel going back in time to show us how they themselves made their riches. *Donned Rags* would see the impoverished **Peter Jones** presenting a new type of Jacuzzi bath with his revolutionary *Jet Openers*, whilst **James Caan** showcases the Bay City Rollers tartan trousers phenomenon – *Macajeans*. **Deborah Meaden** would explain how Ann Summers picked up on *Her Bead Daemon*, and we all know how **Duncan Bannatyne**'s *Canned Banyan Nut* went on to sell millions. But perhaps the most uplifting account of their own humble beginnings comes from **Theo Paphitis** and his campaign for more natural foodstuffs. His campaign '*Eat Hippo Shit*' led to the opening of his first eco-friendly restaurant.

Here's a good line-up of evening television you'd see in Anagramland:

**7.00 PM**  **All Creatures Great and Small**
*Large lads all scatter manure.*

---

**8.00 PM**  **Buffy the Vampire Slayer**
*Fit female, pushy bravery.*

---

**9.00 PM**  **Who Wants to Be a Millionaire?**
*Ah, wow! A time to earn billions.*

---

**10.00 PM**  **The Academy Awards**
*Easy watched drama.*

---

**11.00 PM**  **Footballers' Wives**
*I love fast blowers!*

---

# CELEBRITIES AND ROYALS

Celebrity weddings seem to have taken over the world in the last decade. When it was Elizabeth Taylor and Richard Burton courting, it was big news. Now it's a lifestyle. Ten years ago Ashley Cole was probably playing football on a rough council estate for a hardnosed Sunday League team and Cheryl Tweedy was probably playing football on a rough council estate for a hardnosed Sunday League team. Then they were Mr and Mrs Cole. Then they weren't. Lovely story.

Then there's Brad and Jennifer, Brad and Angelina, Katie and Tom, Catherine and Michael . . . the list goes on and on. The laws of Anagramland would change all of that, with the insistence that you can only marry someone that is an anagram of yourself. Suddenly, your rich and famous celebs are having to slum it with the general public. Fantastic.

So, who would marry whom? Well, I've graded the following into two lists. The A list is those megastars who still do quite well for themselves, marrying into good stock and ending up with someone with whom they are quite happy to be seen out in public. The B list is those who could have done so much better.

# THE A LIST

| CELEBRITY | CLASSY OTHER HALF |
| --- | --- |
| SARAH MICHELLE GELLAR | GRAHAM CHARLES LILLEE |
| NICOLAS CAGE | ELISA COGNAC |
| STEVE MARTIN | VERA MITTENS |
| LIAM NEESON | ELENA SIMON |
| KIM BASINGER | SIR MIKE BANG |
| ELLE MACPHERSON | CHARLES POLEMEN |
| ANNA FRIEL | ALAN FINER |

# THE B LIST

| CELEBRITY | PEASANT |
| --- | --- |
| KIRSTEN DUNST | NED STINKRUST |
| PIERCE BROSNAN | BERNISE CRAPON |
| NATALIE PORTMAN | NIAL TAMPON-TEAR |
| PARIS HILTON | ALI SHITPORN |
| REESE WITHERSPOON | PETER WHORENOISES |
| BRIGITTE NIELSEN | NEIL BIGTITSNEER |

# Royal Family Tree

*(Amorality Freely)*

## Eliza the Queen B

(m. Rub-Fudged Honkie)

### Spear Clincher
(m.1 Landed a Prince, Say)
(m.2 Crablike Llama Powers)

### Nice Spanners
(m.1 Kill Rash Pimp)
(m.2 Lay out the Mincer)

### An Empiric Will
(m. Any UK Mullet)

### Ripple the Lips

### Pry Near Rich

### All Rap His Zip

**Wined Prancer**
(m. & div. Roughness Afar)

**Cidered Prawn**
(m. Enjoys Posh Heirs)

**Scarce Penis Biter**

**Wondrous Day Lilies**

**Insecure Seeping**

**Survives on Cent**

*Answers at the back.*

# Sports Celebrities' DVDs

# REDUCE
# FLOPS

Take Several
Degrees
off Your
Lob Wedge

Golf Education with
# FRED
# COUPLES

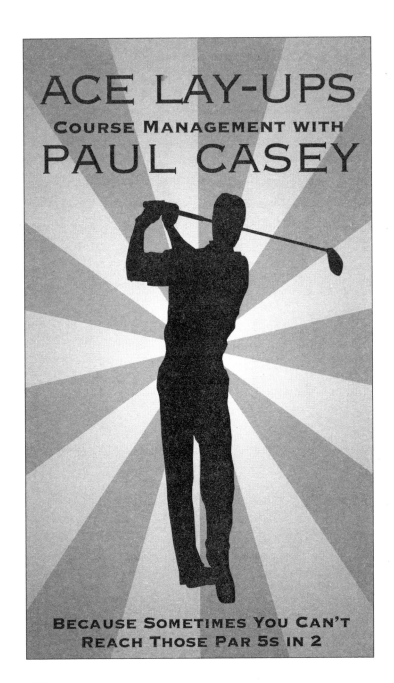

ACE LAY-UPS
COURSE MANAGEMENT WITH
PAUL CASEY

BECAUSE SOMETIMES YOU CAN'T
REACH THOSE PAR 5S IN 2

# WEIRDO TOGS

Why All Golfers
Try to Dress like
Rupert the Bear

## TIGER WOODS

# Scariest
# Grunt

The Ryder Cup legend reveals the moment that
Big John Daly dropped one at the eighteenth
at Augusta.

# Curtis
# Strange

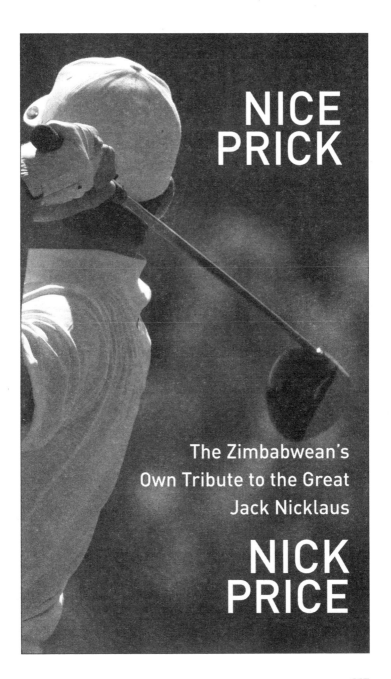

NICE
PRICK

The Zimbabwean's
Own Tribute to the Great
Jack Nicklaus

NICK
PRICE

# LO! MORNING ERECTION

---

## Avoiding Stiffness – the Golfer's Guide to Proper Exercise

---

# COLIN MONTGOMERIE

# FIND HER CLITORIS

*The Olympic Gold Medallist Puts His Finger on the Button*

# LINFORD CHRISTIE

**Warning – Sexually Explicit**
**Contains images of Linford's lunchbox**

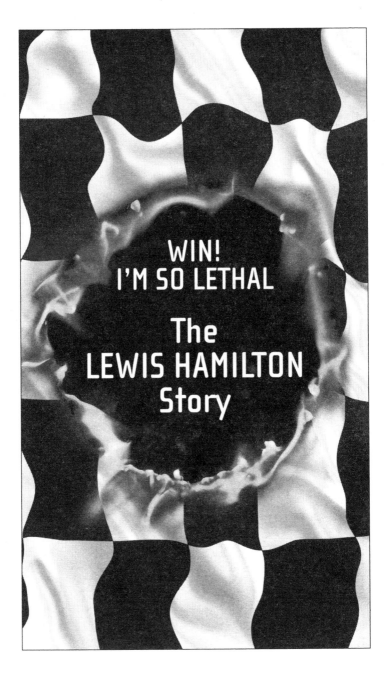

WIN!
I'M SO LETHAL

The
LEWIS HAMILTON
Story

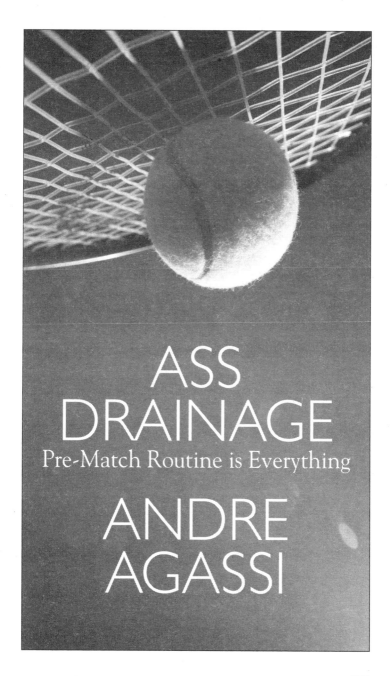

# ASS
# DRAINAGE
Pre-Match Routine is Everything

# ANDRE
# AGASSI

# MAYHEM TO NINTH
From Obscurity to the World's Top Ten

TIMOTHY HENMAN

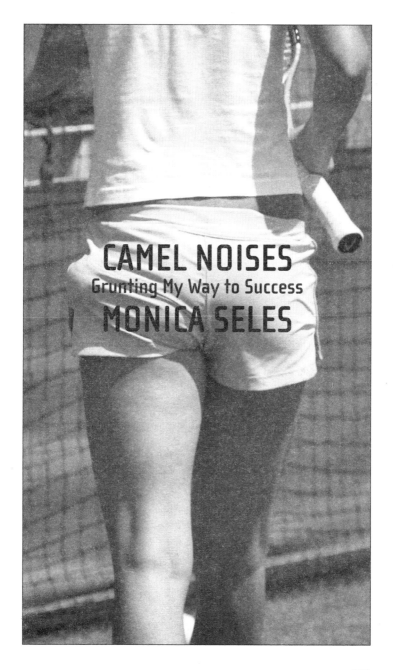

CAMEL NOISES
Grunting My Way to Success
MONICA SELES

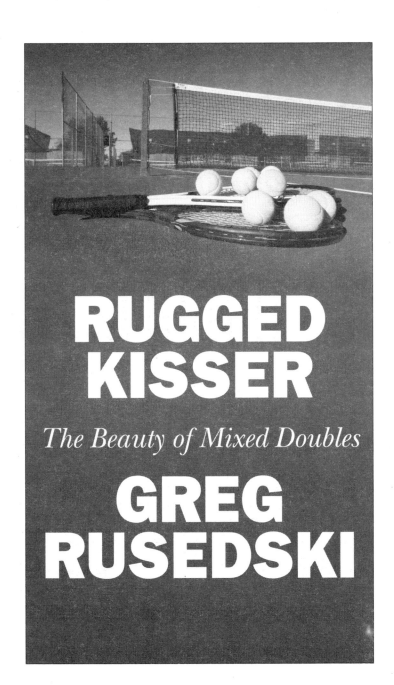

# RUGGED KISSER

*The Beauty of Mixed Doubles*

# GREG RUSEDSKI

# END GOD HELL

**THE EX-ENGLAND MANAGER REVEALS
WHAT THE FA REALLY SAID**

# GLEN
# HODDLE

# Run for Bank
From Vegas to the Dole
## FRANK BRUNO

# HAIL PORTLY PHIL TAYLOR

## Britain's Greatest Ever Athlete?

# Spoonerisms and Other Weird Word Things

# Spoonerisms

'Bosh and Pecks' is a spoonerism for 'Posh and Becks'.

Spoonerisms, which date back to the late nineteenth century, are a form of anagram with usually nonsensical meanings. Their origin is attributed to William Archibald Spooner, Dr Spooner as he became. The Oxford scholar had a nervous speech deficiency, which caused him involuntarily to transpose the initial letters of words to form a muddled and occasionally comical phrase. 'Chish and fips' would be another modern-day example. Such phrases, whether funny or just very stupid, became known as spoonerisms.

When toasting Her Royal Highness, Dr Spooner might have said, 'Here's to the queer old Dean!' Or in a restaurant he might have ordered 'keys and parrots'. Interestingly, Spooner had seven children, so he obviously had great trouble keeping his pilly in his wants.

Sheffield Wednesday would win a football spoonerism league if one existed. Once upon a time they had a midfield consisting of Kenny Lunt, known affectionately at Hillsborough as 'Lenny', alongside the utility man Chris Brunt. Unfortunately they missed the opportunity in the transfer window of signing Willy Sanker and Phil Rucker to complete what would have been a truly memorable central unit. Wednesday fans take great delight, by the way, in referring to ex-Sheffield United manager **Neil Warnock** as *Colin Wanker.*

For spoonerism greatness, though, this has to be the best: I had the pleasure of meeting a lady once who carried the Spooner burden of being called Kerry Hunt. What on earth were the parents thinking? Clearly the careless Hunts had never heard of spoonerisms. Billy old sastards. I wonder if they were both bald.

Other anagram-related linguistic quirks include palindromes (words or phrases that are the same spelt forwards or backwards, e.g. 'Madam') and a semordnilap (an anagram which is a reverse spelling of another word and also comprises a proper phrase – Avid Diva). But let's not go overboard.

# Anagram Elitism

For me, the beauty of the very best anagrams is often in their purity and simplicity – astronomers are *moon starers,* a schoolmaster is in *the classroom* and a gentleman is an *elegant man.* However, there are some people who go to extraordinary lengths to anagrammatise words and phrases and contrive remarkable alternatives to sentences, even paragraphs.

One Cory Calhoun came up with this amazing translation from Shakespeare's *Hamlet*:

> To be, or not to be – that is the question;
> Whether 'tis nobler in the mind to suffer
> The slings and arrows of outrageous fortune

. . . is, believe it or not, an anagram of:

> In one of the Bard's best-thought-of tragedies,
> our insistent hero, Hamlet, queries on two fronts
> about how life turns rotten.

A hundred-letter anagram – I guess it's a bit more sophisticated than my ears and arse.

While not quite as long, one of my own favourites is the anagram of David Beckham and Miss Rebecca Loos: *Bad Soccer Ace Bonks Devilish Madam.*

# Cryptic Clues

I mentioned in the introduction my love of the *Daily Telegraph* crossword. Wordplay is an integral part of cryptic clues, and I have to pay tribute to the person who, one day, presented me with the ultimate in anagram posers:

> Gegs? (9,4)

The solution? Scrambled eggs. Wonderful in its brevity and ingenuity.

# Numbers

Numbers can also be extraordinary. The fact that **111,111,111** multiplied by **111,111,111 = 12,345,678,987,654,321** is amazing, I think, but then I'm not a mathematician.

Linguistically though, the fact that the letter 'A' does not appear in any actual number until the number ONE THOUS<u>A</u>ND is astonishing (excluding the actual word 'and' in between numbers, e.g. 'one hundred and twenty'). I mean, there are an awful lot of As around. 'Anagram' has three of its own, yet the numbers one to nine hundred & ninety-nine have none.

Numbers have a place in Anagramland as well. This remarkable equation is known as an anugram:

### Eleven plus two = twelve plus one.

Not only is the sum of the equation true (13), but the letters on each side are exactly the same (all 13 of them!).

You see; there's much more to anagrams than just swapping a few letters around.

Bet you can't wait for your next dinner party.

# Dr
# Anagram
## #2

PATIENT: Dr Anagram, how are you?

DOCTOR: I'm well, thank you. Oh dear, problem with the back again?

PATIENT: Yes I have. Every time I go to get up, my spine seems to spasm.

DOCTOR: Ah, stiff penis? Very uncomfortable. Tell me, Mr Taylor, is it stiff first thing in the morning?

PATIENT: Very much so, yes. Obviously I've been lying on it all night.

DOCTOR: And does it help if your wife rubs it for a while?

PATIENT: Absolutely, yes, it's much better.

DOCTOR: She's a fine woman your wife. Is everything OK with her arse by the way?

PATIENT: Yes thank you Doctor, the syringing seemed to work wonders. Anyway, see you soon, and thank you for these pills.

# ANIMALS

Let's take a look at Anagramland's animal hierarchy.

It's the **dogs** that are the *gods* and rule our alternative kingdom, with the **cats** as the supporting *cast*. The *big nobs* are the **gibbons**, the **leopards** are the *apelords* and the **donkeys** play the role of *key dons*, whilst the **platypuses** *supply teas*.

**Whales** abide by *she law*, overseen by the *lo admirals*, the **armadillos**, on the *planet She*, the **elephants**.

Animals are crap for anagrams. This is why I just keep fish.

# Musical Collaborations

The earlier chapter on music exposed some new and very different offerings from the world's leading acts. Going one step further and pushing the boundaries of anagram fanaticism to the limit, certain artists could collaborate, purely because of the potential anagrammatic outcome. Enjoy these somewhat unusual joint ventures.

♩ ♪ ♯ ♩ ♩ ♪

### Rachel Stevens/Blue – *The Real S Club Seven*

With Jo O'Meara busy down the bingo, the delectable Ms Stevens calls on a couple of her old band mates (known affectionately as the blonde one and the dark one) and teams up with handsome Duncan, handsome Lee, handsome Simon and Anthony to form the first supergroup of the new millennium. They hope to go down like a Led Zeppelin of modern pop. Just swap the word 'Zeppelin' for 'Balloon' and hey presto!

♩ ♪ ♯ ♩ ♩ ♪

### Gareth Gates/Eminem – *I Engage the Stammer*

Alas, this bizarre duo never gets past the opening track – a cover of Bachman-Turner Overdrive's 'You Ain't Seen Nothing Yet'. Listen in stunned silence as Gates attempts the 'B-b-b-b-b-baby you just ain't seen n-n-n-nothing yet' bit. A week and a half of musical car crashes. Mr Mathers chips in with the occasional 'muthafucker'.

### Blur/Oasis/Pulp – *Labour's Pupils*

The Three Kings of Britpop come together for a Red Rose tribute and what a classic piece of modernist rock 'n' roll it is. The two singles, 'The Gory Tory Story' and the indie war cry 'John Was a Major Twat', give listeners a subtle sense of the theme of this landmark album.

### Mika/Shayne Ward – *I'm a Shady Wanker*

Two of pop's brightest stars get together for an hour of falsetto campness. Go on, on your mum's life, who's the most annoying?

### Dire Straits/Chris Rea – *Artistic Hairdresser*

In a bold attempt to make the dullest record ever, two exponents of the art of tedium combine to bring you forty-five minutes of aural torture in the form of a concept album about a salon owner in Stoke Poges. I won't even bother to make the joke about them renaming the project Dire Rea. Just listen to the umpteen guitar solos and squirm at the painful grimaces as they pluck their G-strings. The final song is entitled 'The Straightener'. Bloody hell.

**Pete Doherty/Kate Moss – *'Me Takes the Dope' Story***

A duet of some substance this – in more ways than one.
A CD of self-examination witnesses the Babyshambles
frontman spurt out more diatribes guaranteed to land
him in hot water and more newspapers. Kate plays the
triangle on 'Flying without Wings'.

**Sting/Leo Sayer – *Tireless Agony***

The only thing worse than 'Roooooooxanne!' is Leo
singing it with that hair.

**Radiohead/Leonard Cohen
– *A Dreaded Hole I Can Honor***

Suicidal tendencies meet morbid depression here, and
fans of wrist-slashing will dig the deep and hidden
meaning behind singalong ditties such as 'The End Is
Nigh', 'Mushroom Sky', 'We're All Gonna Die' and
'Wave Goodbye'. Ideal for christenings and bar mitzvahs.

**U2/McFly/King/Dido – *Fucking My Dildo 2***

Brilliant follow-up to the highly acclaimed debut release, this unlikely quartet once more delivers a heady fusion of classic rock, classic pop, classic long hair and classic boredom.

♪ 𝄢 ♪

**Marillion/Genesis – *Nil Generalissimo***

The one thing that the music world has always feared. Get ready for an hour of adjectival nonsense from Fish and Phil.

Track listing:
The Harlequin's Lament (6.08)
Painting a Teardrop on the Mona Lisa's Visage (9.11)
Light Refraction on a Winter's Morn (7.42)
A Butterfly Flutters in Autumnal Haze (5.58)
Splintering the Remnants of My Shattered Heart (8.16)
Latinum Phrasus to Soundum Cleverus (4.40)
Another Chapter Closes (and the World Sleeps Tonight)
    (12.12)

♪ 𝄢 ♪

# My
# History of
# The
# World

| AD 1 | *Army* gives birth to a little baby *yob* and puts him in a *german*. |
|---|---|
| 1st century | Jesus has a bit of bother with the *Morans*. They *red rum* him. |
| 2nd century | *Ian Hard* built a wall to stop the Jockos heading south. |
| 3rd century | *Moran* Empire up *hits* creek because of *Napier's* threat. |
| 4th century | Attila *He Hunt* registers the earliest claim to Cockney rhyming slang. |
| 5th century | *Den* of the Roman Empire (*stew*). |
| 6th century | Toilet paper invented, so everyone could now wipe their *ears*. |
| 7th century | *Raw*. |
| 8th century | Beowulf has bifters with *Red Glen*. |
| 9th century | The Vikings turn up and begin *grappling and ailing*. |
| 10th century | The Dark *Sage*. |
| 11th century | The Battle of *Shit Nags*, a Grand National for useless horses. |
| 12th century | *Beak the Mascot* killed in Canterbury Cathedral. |
| 13th century | *Anagram Act* sealed at Runnymede and *Macro Loop* reaches *Chain*. |
| 14th century | Hundred Years War begins when Edward III challenges the French *hornet*. |

| | |
|---|---|
| 15th century | Joan of *Car* has a *steak* and Christopher *Bum Locus* sails to America. |
| 16th century | John Harrington invents *T. S. Eliot*. |
| 17th century | *Gawky Fuse* fails to blow up the Houses of *Mental Pair*. |
| 18th century | George *Saw Nothing* becomes first *IT spender* of the US. |
| 19th century | The Lady with the Lamp in the Crimean War – *Leg on Fire, Change Lint!* |
| 20th century | England beats *Meg Ryan*. |
| 21st century | Dan Brown writes *The Dido Vaccine*. |

*Answers at the back.*

# THE OLYMPIC GAMES

**Looser Elastic Band and the Smegma Policy 1220**
Strange sub-heading, eh? If you haven't worked it out by
the anagrammatised date clue, it's the Olympic Games
of 2012. *Looser Elastic Band* is our beloved organiser **Lord
Sebastian Coe**, although I shall shorten that to *Rod Cole*
from now on.

Now I'm a massive fan of the *Smegma Policy* and have
been since *Hasten* in 1896. However, Great Britain rarely
returns with more than a handful of gold medals. All
that is set to change with my radical proposal to Rod
Cole. Let me explain.

As hosts of the Smegma Policy, it should be our
prerogative to include our own novel events in 2012,
thus offering up new opportunities for us to win medals;
the twist being that they must be anagrams of
themselves. For example, I would like to see **Pool** and
*Polo* added to the schedule, two events that we play a lot
of over here and which are both potential medal
chances. I'm not sure about *Water Pool* though – Steve
Davis in Speedos doesn't seem an obvious crowd-pleaser.
However, *White Water Farting* is a certainty.

**Horse Racing** and the relatively unknown sport of
*Orc Shearing* would be next on the list; the Sport of Kings
definitely presents a medal opportunity for Great
Britain, as long as some of our jockeys are still at large,
but we would face tough competition from the Anzacs in
the Orc Shearing. Still on an equestrian theme, the
**Steeplechase** would run on the same day as my
controversial suggestion of *Cheese Plates*, a contest that
would showcase all that's great about world cheeses.
Confidence would be high with the patriotic cheddar,
but you'd have to fancy the Dutch gouda and Italian
gorgonzola to test our very strongest yellow portion. Of

course, the French would arrive laden with talent in the shape of brie and camembert and a lot of people will have a few quid each way on the Bavarian smoked, having done so well for the Germans in the Europeans last year. If you're looking at outsiders, the Danish blue at 33/1 could be worth a sniff, but a little wager on the *chad red* at 50/1 could well pay dividends.

Why *chad red*? **Cheddar** of course!

**Volleyball** is always a popular event, and I believe would increase in popularity with the addition of my new sport, *Lovely Ball*, the winner of which would be the man with the most beautiful teste and would be judged, like gymnastics, by an expert panel. Home favourite Dicky 'Smoothnut' McPherson would be looking for a 9.8 or better, but would be strongly challenged by the well-known German, Michael Bollock.

The **Decathlon** and the *Hot Candle* (a kind of adult egg-and-spoon race, but with wax and bondage tape) would also be compulsory viewing, as well as **Water Skiing** and *Stake Wiring*, an event that will have erectors of tents tuned in nightly. I am fully expecting my last two suggestions to be turned down, however, unless the International Olympic Committee agree to screen them after the 9.00pm watershed.

**Ice Skating**, I propose, should be held alongside *Sick Eating*, and **Trap Shooting** will end the Games with *Tarts Poohing*, surely a better and more memorable conclusion than all that flag-waving nonsense. I'd back the Dumping Danes for glory in this one.

I don't expect ever to hear back from Rod. Having said that, perhaps he'll like my final idea that girls that play in the **Netball** competition must be *All Bent*.

# FOOD

**Waiter:** Good evening and welcome to
L'Anagramme. Are you ready to order, sir? I
should let you know we do 'ave a few items
off the menu tonight, but we 'ave many
replacement dishes also.

**Customer:** Fine. I'll start with the Pate on Toast please.

**Waiter:** I'm afraid the pate, he is not available, sir.

**Customer:** Well what do you have instead?

**Waiter:** Ant Potatoes. Zey are leedle tiny potatoes
'arvested by trained ants.

**Customer:** What about Dressed Whole Crab?

**Waiter:** We do not currently 'ave any. Instead I can
offer you Beardless Chowder. Iss a bowl of

delicious chowder, which our chef 'e 'as lovingly shaved.

**Customer:** No, I'm fine. Let's just move on to the main courses. Do you have the Roast Chicken?

**Waiter:** No.

**Customer:** Well what do you have?

**Waiter:** Chronic Steak.

**Customer:** Don't think I fancy that. Roast Turkey?

**Waiter:** Kraut Oyster.

**Customer:** Beef Wellington?

**Waiter:** No, but I can offer you instead Leg of Belin Newt.

**Customer:** This is ridiculous. Do you have anything on the menu? Salmon en Croûte?

**Waiter:** Courtesan Melon.

**Customer:** Atlantic Lobster?

**Waiter:** Cat in Otter's Ball.

**Customer:** Steak and Mushroom Pie!

**Waiter:** Seasoned Hokum Armpit.

**Customer:** Look, can I just have some bread and butter please?

**Waiter:** Ze bread and butter, 'e 'as gone. But I can offer you Tuned, Barbed Rat?

**Customer:** That sounds wonderful. We'll have two of those.

# THEATRE

You cannot beat a night at the theatre. Unless you like paintball. Make sure you get tickets for the following alternative stage plays:

## *Toad Prompts*

—by—

# Tom Stoppard

Told from the perspective of a man whose job it is to make sure toads make noises at the right point in nature programmes, this very different production questions our understanding of language, time, nature, culture, guilt, innocence, love, loss and frogs. Four hours long with no interval.

*Rewarded Nobby Well*
~by~
Andrew Lloyd Webber

Wee Nobby Barnes comes from a broken home with no real
prospects for the future. Then, on a life-changing Sunday
morning at his local village fête, Nobby meets Maurice, a
morris-dancing enthusiast. Nobby joins Maurice's morris
dancers and they unexpectedly win the area championships
and thus go on to represent the county in the National
Finals. Heart-warming, sad and at times extremely comical,
*Rewarded Nobby Well* is this year's *Billy Elliot*, but with slightly
stranger dance scenes. Vinnie Jones, making his stage debut
as Maurice, is quite magnificent.

## I'll Hurt 'Er Arm

~by~

# Arthur Miller

A rare outing for this early Miller play about Tony, a rough-and-ready market worker who can only communicate through Chinese burns. Leslie Grantham makes a wholly unwelcome return to the entertainment industry.

## A Sweetness Ill in Me

~by~

# Tennessee Williams

Small Southern town. The hottest night of the year. A sweaty woman left wandering about in her nightie, tormented by her ex-lover's ghost. That actually sounds pretty good. Put me down for a couple of tickets. Maybe four.

## Nor a Beggared Shrew

~by~

# George Bernard Shaw

'I am not a harridan, sir, nor a virago, no, nor a beggared shrew either, whatever they may say about me.' Another play with people laughing at things that aren't funny any more just to prove they went to university. Apparently you pronounce his middle name to rhyme with *canard*? I'm off to watch *Celebrity Wife Swap*.

## IT Crime

~by~

# Tim Rice

Spamming, hacking and identity theft, all set to a stunning musical score. 'Phantom of the Opera Browser' will leave you aghast.

# *I'm Anarchy Elf*

*by*

# Michael Frayn

Groundbreaking pantomime from England's foremost dramatist. Anarchy Elf wants to bring down the patriarchal hegemony of capitalism by destroying Christmas. He is helped by Engels the reindeer and a surprising ally in a red suit.

# *Fuehrer's Unhealthy Pig*

*by*

# Stephen Fry/Hugh Laurie

A kind of *Great Escape* meets *Babe* political satire that will have you nodding your head in appreciation of Fry's astonishing intelligence and knowledge of the Third Reich. Jade Goody makes her long-awaited stage debut.

## *Knob Fever Fest*

~by~

# Steven Berkoff

TOTAL THEATRE MY ARSE! This is *Saturday Night Fever* meets *The Romans in Britain* – without the dancing. And the white suits.

## *Onlineism*

~by~

# Neil Simon

Love in cyberspace is the inspiration for Neil's modern-day take on internet dating. The curtain opens on a virtual dinner party where six strangers from different parts of the world gather for an e-feast. Clever, dangerous and extraordinarily erotic. Watch out for the thin Finn and the brûlée. Makes *9½ Weeks* look like an episode of *Ready Steady Cook*.

# THE DAILY ANAGRAM

As we all know, the **tabloid press** are s*poiled brats* and can be over the top, particularly in their insistence at putting '-gate' at the end of every scandal. Personally, I'm praying for some sort of toothpaste scandal so we can have Colgategate. However, I love some aspects of newspaper sensationalism. Some of the tabloids produce some genuinely fantastic headlines, and in Anagramland, the press would not be disappointed.

## Alternative news sources

**New York Times – Monkeys Write**
**Manchester Evening News – Event Searching Newsmen**
**News of the World – Wrote Down Flesh**
**Daily Telegraph – Heated Playgirl**
**Sunday Times – Massed Unity**
**Daily Express – Spread Sexily**
**Financial Times – Inflict Amnesia**
**Sunday Telegraph – Naughty Pleaders**
**The Observer – Severe Throb**
**Sunday People – Openly Paused**
**Evening Standard – Ends Vagina Trend**
**The Scotsman – Mash Contest**

Or readers could turn to the *Daily Anagram* for their news. Here, I've taken a person's name and jumbled the letters to form the headline-grabbing story . . .

# ROYAL

## Princess Anne – *Nice Spanners!*

Queen over the moon with Princess Royal's new tools

There was great **DELIGHT** at Buckingham Palace yesterday as HRH Princess Anne unveiled her new set of **SPANNERS** to the world.

## THE MALL

Thousands flooded down The Mall to see the event, and the general consensus was that it was indeed a lovely set of spanners, superseding Prince Charles's fine collection of chisels as the nation's favourite royal tools. A source close to the princess said, 'She's really glad that she can finally come out from under the shadow of Charles's equipment and really show the world her spanners.'

# SPORT

## Sandra Bullock *Rounds Ballack*

Keanu believe it! *Speed* star shows Kraut skipper up as
Yank girls stuff the Hun

In one of the great footballing **SHOCKS** of all time, the
United States women's team last night knocked out the
mighty German men's team after a scheduling **ERROR**.
Trailing 1–0 from a Schweinsteiger, 24, free-kick early in
the first half, the US women's team rallied late on and
equalised with an own goal by defender Philipp Lahm, 26.
Then with just minutes remaining, Bullock, 44, latched on
to a long clearance from the American goalkeeper, 31.
With the German defence, 125, still upfield from the
preceding corner, only skipper Michael Ballack, 31, stood
between Sandra and the goal. With a series of Cristiano
Ronaldo-type step-overs, the actress bemused Ballack and
left him dead on the ground, shouting '*Gott in Himmel!*' as
Sandra thrashed the ball past a helpless Jens Lehmann, 38,
to put the US women's team into the semi-finals.

## Sir Alex Ferguson *in Sex-Slag Furore*

United Boss to fight carnal custard claims

Manchester United manager Sir Alex Ferguson was last
night at the centre of an extraordinary lawsuit involving
twin sisters and a really big tin of Ambrosia. Ferguson is
normally at his most excitable when rapidly chewing gum
and tapping his watch in the fourth minute of stoppage
time. But in soon-to-be-published photographs, the Scot
has allegedly been pictured with the twins covered in a
creamy-type pudding, wearing nothing but a contented
grin, while masticating furiously.

# POLITICS

## George W. Bush *Buggers Howe*

### Geoffrey Howe **ACCIDENTALLY** bummed by most powerful man on earth

Calls were building last night for an investigation into how George W. Bush became involved in what the State Department last night was calling 'a freak trouser incident'.

'I had just popped out to do some shopping in my local store,' explains Geoffrey. 'I'd parked the car a little crookedly, because I'm old and stupid and as I went to feed the meter, I dropped a pound coin on the pavement and, I don't know, he must have slipped and accidentally pulled both of our trousers off. Well you just don't expect that kind of thing to happen in such a quiet village.' A local Conservative spokesperson called for an investigation into how this would affect house prices in the area.

# ENTERTAINMENT

## Simon Cowell *Comes on Will*
Judge jizzes live on heir!

In a special royal version of *The X Factor* shown last night, show mastermind Simon Cowell ejaculated on the heir to the throne, following his epic performance of Whigfield's 'Saturday Night'. Even Cowell's notoriously high trousers could not prevent Simon's semen sailing towards the stage, landing on the gushing prince. William fought off stiff competition from Prince Andrew and his unusual version of Metallica's 'Enter Sandman', and Fergie, supported as always by the Black-Eyed Peas.

## Alyssa Milano*'s a Noisy Llama*

Neighbours of Hollywood superstar Alyssa Milano, 36, were last night in uproar after they were yet again kept awake by her night-time antics. The troubled singer has reportedly been heard SPITTING, CHEWING CUD and DOING OTHER THINGS LLAMAS DO.

Bill Parsons, who has lived in the same road for forty years, explains, 'Honestly, she goes at it like billy-o for hours on end. It really is like listening to a llama.'

## Yasmine Bleeth – '*The Lesbiany Me*'

In an exclusive interview, former *Baywatch* star Yasmine Bleeth, 40, **EXPLAINS** how she is not 'a full-on lesbian, not one of those scary ones who don't like men at all, but if there are boys watching and I've had a couple of glasses of Jacob's Creek, I sometimes go a bit lesbiany and that'.

# CARAMELIERI

Anagramland's Magazine of the Year

## EDITORIAL
Editor in Chief – Frenchie Idiot
Deputy Editor – Dottie Duprey
Features Writer – Frere Watersuit
Chief Reporter – Cherrie Profet
Reporter – Peter Orr
Sub-Editor – Doris Tube

## MARKETING
Special Projects – Jesper Coatclips
Marketing Manager – Annika Eggtrammer
Marketing Manager – Margaret Nameking

## SUBSCRIPTIONS
Subscriptions – Ross Pubic-Nits
Subscriptions – Scot Piss-Bruin
Circulation – Carlio Cunti

**Where a stupid, slightly foreign-sounding name
may well get you a job**

# Dr Anagram

# #3

PATIENT: Hello Doctor, I wonder if you can point me in the right direction.

DOCTOR: I'll try, Mr Matthews, what is it exactly?

PATIENT: Well I know it sounds a bit vain, Doctor, but I'm thinking of having some cosmetic surgery and I was hoping you could recommend somebody.

DOCTOR: I'm sure I can, what is it that you want to have done? Not looking at a spine extension, are you?

PATIENT: No, no, that's all fine. It's more of a facial thing really, I'd like to try and slim my face down and highlight my cheekbones more. What do you think?

DOCTOR: Nothing wrong with your knobcheese in my opinion.

PATIENT: Well thank you Doctor, but I want more prominent cheekbones you see. I always notice cheekbones on people's faces.

DOCTOR: Yes yes, I know what you mean. Well, I know a superb knobcheese specialist. Here's his card.

# CRICKET

If ever an ex-sportsman was destined to go into television presenting, it has to be Somerset's **Marcus Trescothick**, his surname being a very cute anagram of *Cricket Host*, as well as *Cricket Shot* in fact. No wonder we lost the last Ashes series without him. But then again we did have **Duncan Fletcher** in charge and any man who appears in Anagramland as *Unclenched Fart* is perhaps not the man to inspire the lads against the might of the Green and Gold.

In order to win back that little urn, we'd need to field the following all-time Cricketing Anagram Fantasy XI. See if you can guess them.

I'l Anchor The Team

Recto Toffee Bogey

Wrestle A Cat

Heal Much Vagina (*I cat nap*)

I Invent Keepers

Him On A Bat

Rejoins Agent (*Peeker*)

Bastard Tour

Randiest Tomboy

A Porn Amnesty

Massive Throne

Or how about this for a World XI?

Ginger Green Dodo (I Witnessed)

Pony Tricking (A US Lariat)

You Madam of Mush (Pasta Ink)

Enchilada Trunks (I and I)

Desirable Frogs (I Witnessed)

Horny Dreams (A US Lariat)

Relevant Idiot (Daze en Lawn)

Wears Henna (A US Lariat)

Alcohol Spunk (Safari Touch)

Raunchy Towels (I Witnessed)

Bleary Scrotum (I Witnessed)

*Answers at the back.*

You have to admit; it's a terrifying thought facing Bleary Scrotum with a new ball, followed by one that lifts sharply from Raunchy Towels. On a turning pitch, you may be outdone by Alcohol Spunk's googly or a wrong 'un from the Relevant Idiot, whilst Horny Dreams will continually try to whip your bails off from behind. All painful stuff.

# DR
# ANAGRAM
## #4

A man walks in with a racket, clutching his arm.

DOCTOR:     Tennis Bowel. Goodbye.

# HARRY POTTER

Forget the Philosopher's Stone and the Chamber of Secrets; these would be much more fun.

## Harry Potter and the Sheepish Poltroons

In this opening chapter of the anagrammatised collection, the wand-waving wizard takes on a bunch of nervous cowards – and loses.

## Harry Potter and Beasts from the Crèche

In the second instalment of the sorcery series, young Harry battles with a bunch of out-of-control three-year-olds. He loses.

## Harry Potter and the Zebras of Anion Park

The Gryffindor great is no match for the negatively charged stripy chaps.

## Harry Potter and the Fleet of Gorbi

One-way traffic from start to finish as the mighty Russians easily overpower Harry, Ron and the blossoming Hermione.

$$\oint$$

## Harry Potter and the Hexed Rhino Poofter

Slightly less subtle about sexuality in this book than Rowling was with Dumbledore. Although they'll still say the rhino isn't gay in some US states.

$$\oint$$

## Harry Potter and the Childproof Bean

Overrun this time by a broad bean that had already defeated one of the Beasts from the Crèche, the bespectacled genius comes really unstuck.

$$\oint$$

## Harry Potter and the Lethal Shady Owl

A sad demise for Potter, as he continues his abysmal away record with a comprehensive defeat against his own nasty pet.

# Harry Potter Spin-Offs

Get set for a whole load of moneymaking spin-offs featuring these famous Potter protagonists.

### Her Orange Minger
**Hermione Granger** narrates a ninety-minute soliloquy about the love of her life, ginger Ron.

### A Sneery Owl
Meanwhile the orange minger, **Ron Weasley**, adopts his own mocking bird.

### Lorded Usable Bum
The ghost of 'outed' headmaster **Albus Dumbledore** offers up his wares.

### His Guru Beard
**Rubeus Hagrid**, the hairy one, turns prophet.

### Vague Old Loon
**Luna Lovegood** looks into the future and sees . . . herself.

### Dark Nosy Phantom
**Nymphadora Tonks** comes face to face with Professor Snape in the afterlife.

# BOOKS

Only in the world of interrogation by anagram could the great **William Shakespeare** openly declare, '*I am a Weakish Speller*', **Charlotte Brontë** admit to being a *Tolerant Botcher* and **Charles Dickens** confide that he felt his work *Lacked Richness*. More recently, **Will Self** has derided a piece of his own as '*Elf Swill*', but then he's only ever a rogue apostrophe and space from owning his own elf. He's a bit like **Hilary Swank** that way. Such is the power of the mixed-up word to reveal all that is hidden.

Authors are vulnerable like anyone else to the variation of letters, and on the next few pages you will see some very famous scribes alongside their appropriately anagrammatised works.

## Catherine Cookson – *Coronation Cheeks*

Beautiful novel about the life of Yorkshire farm girl Mary Higginbotham. Mary dreams of being a princess and eventually queen of England. Tracing her family heritage and a previously unknown historical bloodline, she does indeed become queen. To celebrate she shows the watching world her buttocks.

## Martina Cole – *Reclamation*

Abused by her father, successful businesswoman Chloe Stevenson revisits the ghosts of her past to reclaim the teenage years she never had. Talks are already under way for a made-for-television adaptation starring Dervla Kirwan and the McGann brothers, as none of them has done anything for a few days.

## Martin Amis – *Imam Strain*

Martin sets out his reasoned argument for why all Muslims in Great Britain should be cryogenically frozen in carbonite, like Han Solo in *The Empire Strikes Back.*

## Sidney Sheldon – *Ended Holy Sins*

Some rich bird called Melissa or Sheridan, who has just inherited four billion big ones from her daddy's publishing empire, will meet a handsome young priest called Daniel. She will enjoy the smooth stroking motions of his manhood; he will enjoy her ample bosoms and her heaps of wonga, until she discovers the secret of her father's death – he did it. Bugger. Back to the confession box, Danny Boy.

## Yann Martel – *Mental Yarn*

In the long-awaited follow-up to *Life of Pi*, Yann once more spends a hundred pages confusing the life out of the reader before sending us all on a hallucinatory journey with a horny badger, a goat, a stoat and a trumpet-playing gorilla. But they were really only chess pieces – or something like that. Just pretend you know what the fuck it was all about the next time somebody clever asks you at a dinner party. Use phrases such as 'extraordinary depth', 'infectious dialogue' and 'juxtaposition of storylines' before legging it to the bog to hide your Sidney Sheldon collection.

## Zadie Smith – *Midsize Hat*

Between writing a series of articles on Ukrainian folk art, the introduction to an anthology of bee poetry and judging the indoor Commonwealth pole-vault, Zadie finds time to knock out a novel about a hat that is neither too big nor too small.

## Audrey Niffenegger – *Iffy Underage Genre*

Sequel to the slightly disturbing *The Time Traveler's Wife*. This time old Audrey has an octogenarian actress infatuated with an eight-year-old schoolboy. Ten minutes later they're both thirty and engaged, but then the eighty-four-year-old sees herself at thirty jumping off the top of a building. Strange, beautiful and a little bit pervy. Pulitzer-bound I'm sure. They like a bit of kinky stuff.

## Lynne Truss – *Sly Stunner*

Exiting sequel too *Eats Shoots and Leaves*, about a female spy. Its full of twist's and turn's. The seen were an acomoddating bad guy reveals there plan for world domination is grate.

## Michael Palin – *A Pill Machine*

While on his annual global jolly, the intrepid comedy genius discovers a revolutionary device that gives out free antihistamines to hay fever sufferers in Iceland. The scene in which Palin meets the sneezers from the geysers is moving beyond belief.

## James Patterson – *A Jester's Tampon*

The four-hundred-and-seventy-third Alex Cross novel sees the heroic detective facing every imaginable demon in the world, including a female harlequin, who despite having her period can still swim, run and juggle a load of balls. Each chapter is only forty lines long, so you'll be on chapter 100 on about page 98, when the big twist comes. It's his colleague. Well blow me down.

## Oscar Wilde – *Coward's Lie*

Me and Noel, we were just good friends . . .

## Abi Titmuss – *Ass Bum Titi*

This is a warm autobiographical account of the busty ex-nurse's rise to stardom, and the title is a fine introduction to this outstanding literary debut. The seventeen pages of text blend seamlessly with the 262 topless glamour shots. Expect a video any minute now.

## Kate Mosse – *So Stake Me!*

After her first two novels, Kate changes direction in this light-hearted exploration of a woman whose sassy teenage daughter turns out to be a vampire.

## Sharon Osbourne – *Baroness Honour*

Warts-and-all autobiography from the only woman in the world with Botoxed feet. The book traces her rise from Mrs Ozzy to Baroness Sharon and beyond. Plenty of *X Factor* references and secrets about Simon and 'the other one' should guarantee this a place on the bestseller lists for some while.

## Jodi Picoult – *Judo Politic*

Jodi turns her roving eye on a family torn apart by whose turn it is to take the kids to judo practice. It's so now, somehow.

## Gordon Ramsay – *My Gonads Roar*

Typically controversial, yet always entertaining, the outspoken TV chef explains how expressive his own testicles are. 'It's simple,' proffers Ramsay. 'My bollocks are just really spunky. Fucking hell.'

## Ben Elton – *Le Bonnet*

Roguish Ben writes a book about a cap found in Marseilles which causes wearers to speak very quickly about important political issues.

## Michael Palin – *Neil MacPhail*

During another transcontinental sojourn, the Python legend comes across an Australian man who can put his head up his own arse. Three hundred pages of extraordinary stories, although the photos are confusing, as one never gets a really good look at Mr MacPhail's face.

## Gerald Seymour

A collection of his best short stories:

*Measured Glory* – Immerse yourself in enigmatic espionage

*Rogered Asylum* – Government conspiracy to send all Johnny Foreigners home

*My Regular Dose* – Page-turning drug-smuggling thriller

*Gruesomer Lady* – Ruth Ellis is reincarnated in modern-day London

*Armoury Sledge* – Welcome to the new weapon of worldly destruction

*Roguery Medals* – A story of fiendish disguise and wartime tomfoolery

## Sophie Kinsella – *Pinhole-like Ass*

What if you woke up and you had a really small bumhole? How would you poo? What might it look like? Wholemeal spaghetti? Old-fashioned postal string? More twenty-first-century chick-lit asking the questions that matter.

## Vladimir Nabokov – *Vivid Amoral Bonk*

Long-lost follow-up to the controversial *Lolita* continues with the son of Humbert Humbert, Humbert Humbert Humbert, carrying on the stark, perverted and no less illegal deeds of his old man.

## Minette Walters – *Neil Met Stewart*

What happens when two strangers get into a lift and it breaks down? This outstanding thriller centres on the growing tension that builds between the two characters in the hot, claustrophobic elevator. When the lift does eventually arrive at the ground floor, the doors open and Neil is lying dead on the floor and Stewart is covered in blood, holding a pair of scissors. As whodunits go, this is right up there.

## Jeremy Clarkson – *Only Cars Jerk Me*

Toyota, Opel, Saab, Skoda, E-type, Renault.

## John Grisham – *Harming Josh*

Six-year-old Josh Bender is the only witness to the murder of a Mafia hit man. You know the rest. Tom Cruise will be in the film.

## Agatha Christie – *Ah! Airtight Case*

A train, a man with a limp and a briefcase stolen from the overnight locker – it's all contained in yet another Belgian detective whodunit. Prefer Kojak personally.

## J. K. Rowling – *Owl King Jr*

A kind of cross between *The Lion King* and Harry's white owl, this is a somewhat confusing affair.

## Khaled Hosseini – *Sheikh Is 'No Deal'*

With only two boxes left – the 10p and the £20,000 – the richest man in the world turns down the banker's offer of £6,500. Leon Edmonds narrates the audio book.

## Conn Iggulden – *Dunce Longing*

A change in pace from his collection of trivia for listless middle managers and various historical gore-fests, this book takes us on the emotional journey of what it's like to fancy stupid people.

## Ernest Hemingway – *The Sinewy German*

1916. Ypres. A thin bloke from Hamburg.

## Hugh Fearnley-Whittingstall
### *– Heart, Leg, Thigh, Willy, Anus 'n' Ft*

The quirky cooky explains, categorically, how to eat each and every part of a dead beast.

## Enid Blyton – *Tiny Blonde*

When Kylie Minogue hired the much-loved dead children's novelist to ghost-write her biography, many were surprised at the cute Australian's choice. But after reading chapter 8, which involves Michael Hutchence and Timmy the dog, you will wonder no longer. Brilliant.

## Kathy Reichs – *The Hayricks*

Forensic anthropologist Savannah Hart is called to the grisly scene of a toe bone found in a barn on a Detroit farm. From the one-inch discovery, and with the help of handsome FBI stalwart Bunk McCarthy, Savannah concludes that the victim is male, Caucasian, six foot two, 212 pounds, lived in East Grinstead and was a big fan of Mott the Hoople and banana crazy milk. The two protagonists may come close to snogging, but won't quite.

## Peter Ackroyd – *Created Porky*

A terribly honest and revealing autobiography.

## Henning Mankell – *Hangmen in Knell*

The best thing to come out of Sweden since Benny and Björn, Mankell delivers a classic murder mystery involving some meatballs and one of IKEA's 'easy to assemble' chests of drawers.

## Albert Camus – *Macabre Lust*

Three hundred pages of highly dubious behaviour, but all the bondage and gimp-masks are fine because it's existentialist. That Sartre fella was the same – dirty bugger, but no worries, 'Our destiny is governed by actions.' Tell that to your mum next time she opens the door without knocking.

## Michael Ondaatje – *The Olde Jamaican*

*The English Patient* was remarkable, mainly because it went on all day and featured a man in a bed for much of the time. This follow-up is much more interesting, depicting the life of a washed-up reggae star who travels back through time to medieval England and invents Supermalt.

## Delia Smith – *Meals I'd Hit*

Hip-hop fan Delia's newest bestseller lists the meals that are so easy to make she'd have sex with them.

### Rose Tremain – *Remonterais*

The resurgence, the uprising, the Bastille – French stuff. Gérard Depardieu. *Je voudrais un pamplemousse.*

### Michael Palin – *Cinema Phalli*

Whilst spending an unnecessary amount of the licence-payers' money drinking the finest Italian wine in Sorrento, Mick the Stick pops into the local theatre to watch a film about Roman cocks.

### Robert Ludlum – *Bullet or Drum*

The ultimate rollercoaster. It's all here, so sit tight! Muscovites, Shiites, Satanic rites, religious fights, megabytes, Templar Knights, the Barron Knights, fishnet tights, Bird's Eye Chicken Bites, Miller Lites, Diamond Whites, Diamond Lights, Hoddle, Waddle and a whole load of twaddle from the master of the fucking complicated. The book title will have nothing whatsoever to do with the storyline, it will just add to your total bemusement.

## Thomas Harris – *Hashram Riots*

That nasty Hannibal man returns to haunt our dreams once more, this time turning up during some local unrest in Saudi Arabia. No bother though, ever-civilised Lecter kills all those revolting with a ladle and then eats their ears with some garlic ghee. One to read to the kiddies on a lovely spring day.

## Dan Brown – *Brown Dan*

*Cheat, Divide, Con.* A couple of sodding anagrams, that's all. It's not a whole book, is it?

# ANSWERS

# The Alternative England Anagram Football XI

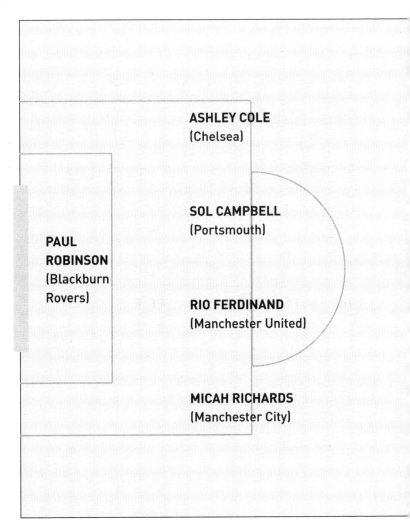

**ASHLEY COLE**
(Chelsea)

**SOL CAMPBELL**
(Portsmouth)

**PAUL ROBINSON**
(Blackburn Rovers)

**RIO FERDINAND**
(Manchester United)

**MICAH RICHARDS**
(Manchester City)

*Substitutes*:
**Shaun Wright-Phillips** (Chelsea)
**Ben Foster** (Manchester United)

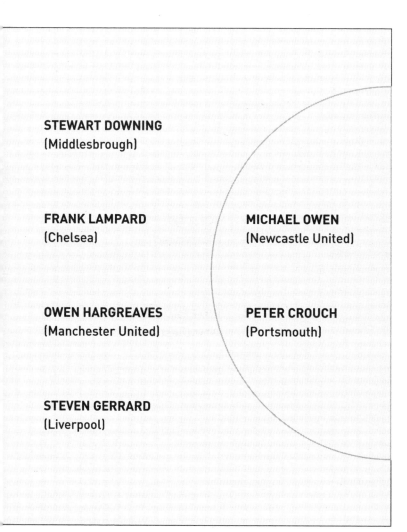

**STEWART DOWNING**
(Middlesbrough)

**FRANK LAMPARD**
(Chelsea)

**MICHAEL OWEN**
(Newcastle United)

**OWEN HARGREAVES**
(Manchester United)

**PETER CROUCH**
(Portsmouth)

**STEVEN GERRARD**
(Liverpool)

**Gareth Barry** (Aston Villa)
**Ashley Young** (Aston Villa)
**Wayne Rooney** (Manchester United)

# PREMIERSHIP TABLE 2007/2008

| Pos | Team |
| --- | --- |
| 1 | Manchester United |
| 2 | Chelsea |
| 3 | Arsenal |
| 4 | Liverpool |
| 5 | Everton |
| 6 | Aston Villa |
| 7 | Blackburn Rovers |
| 8 | Portsmouth |
| 9 | Manchester City |
| 10 | West Ham United |
| 11 | Tottenham Hotspur |
| 12 | Newcastle United |
| 13 | Middlesbrough |
| 14 | Wigan Athletic |
| 15 | Sunderland |
| 16 | Bolton Wanderers |
| 17 | Fulham |
| 18 | Reading |
| 19 | Birmingham City |
| 20 | Derby County |

| | |
| --- | --- |
| Spain: | Barcelona |
| Italy: | Inter Milan |
| Germany: | Bayern Munich |
| Holland: | Sparta Rotterdam |
| France: | Paris Saint Germain |
| Portugal: | Sporting Lisbon |
| Belgium: | Brugge |

| Manager | Ground |
| --- | --- |
| Sir Alex Ferguson | Old Trafford |
| Avram Grant | Stamford Bridge |
| Arsène Wenger | Emirates Stadium |
| Rafa Benítez | Anfield |
| David Moyes | Goodison Park |
| Martin O'Neill | Villa Park |
| Mark Hughes | Ewood Park |
| Harry Redknapp | Fratton Park |
| Sven Goran Eriksson | City of Manchester Stadium |
| Alan Curbishley | Upton Park |
| Juande Ramos | White Hart Lane |
| Kevin Keegan | St James' Park |
| Gareth Southgate | Riverside Stadium |
| Steve Bruce | JJB Stadium |
| Roy Keane | Stadium of Light |
| Gary Megson | Reebok Stadium |
| Roy Hodgson | Craven Cottage |
| Steve Coppell | Madejski Stadium |
| Alex McLeish | St Andrews |
| Paul Jewell | Pride Park |

# Top Ten Countries

Argentina
Bangladesh
South Africa
Cameroon
Singapore
El Salvador
The Gambia
United Arab Emirates
The Maldives
Côte d'Ivoire

# Royal Family Tree

Queen Elizabeth
(m. Duke of Edinburgh)

Prince Charles
(m.1 Lady Diana Spencer)          Prince William
(m.2 Camilla Parker Bowles)       Prince Harry

Princess Anne                     Peter Phillips
(m.1 Mark Phillips)               (m. Autumn Kelly)
(m.2 Timothy Laurence)            Zara Phillips

Prince Andrew                     Princess Beatrice
(m. & div. Sarah Ferguson)        Princess Eugenie

Prince Edward                     Lady Louise Windsor
(m. Sophie Rhys-Jones)            Viscount Severn

# My History of the World

| | |
|---|---|
| AD 1 | Mary gives birth to a little baby boy and puts him in a manger. |
| 1st century | Jesus has a bit of bother with the Romans. They murder him. |
| 2nd century | Hadrian built a wall to stop the Jockos heading south. |
| 3rd century | Roman Empire up shit creek because of Persian threat. |
| 4th century | Attila the Hun registers the earliest claim to Cockney rhyming slang. |
| 5th century | End of the Roman Empire (west). |
| 6th century | Toilet paper invented, so everyone could now wipe their arse. |
| 7th century | War. |
| 8th century | Beowulf has bifters with Grendel. |
| 9th century | The Vikings turn up and begin raping and pillaging. |
| 10th century | The Dark Ages. |
| 11th century | The Battle of Hastings, a Grand National for useless horses. |
| 12th century | Thomas à Becket killed in Canterbury Cathedral. |
| 13th century | Magna Carta sealed at Runnymede and Marco Polo reaches China. |
| 14th century | Hundred Years War begins when Edward III challenges the French throne. |
| 15th century | Joan of Arc has a stake and Christopher Columbus sails to America. |
| 16th century | John Harrington invents toilets. |
| 17th century | Guy Fawkes fails to blow up the Houses of Parliament. |
| 18th century | George Washington becomes first president of the US. |
| 19th century | The Lady with the Lamp in the Crimean War – Florence Nightingale. |
| 20th century | England beats Germany. |
| 21st century | Dan Brown writes *The Da Vinci Code*. |

# Cricket

## England

Michael Atherton

Geoffrey Boycott

Alec Stewart

Michael Vaughan (*Captain*)

Kevin Pietersen

Ian Botham

Geraint Jones (*Keeper*)

Stuart Broad

Ryan Sidebottom

Monty Panesar

Steve Harmison

## World XI

Gordon Greenidge (West Indies)

Ricky Ponting (Australia)

Mohammad Yousuf (Pakistan)

Sachin Tendulkar (India)

Garfield Sobers (West Indies)

Rodney Marsh (Australia)

Daniel Vettori (New Zealand)

Shane Warne (Australia)

Shaun Pollock (South Africa)

Courtney Walsh (West Indies)

Curtly Ambrose (West Indies)

# The Serious Gape,
# I Mean Page

**Thank you to:**

Every single person in this book who is blessed with the necessary combination of vowels and consonants to enable me to recreate his or her existence.

Jamie Coleman at Toby Eady Associates.

Henry Volans, John Grindrod, Julian Loose, Dave Watkins and Rebecca Pearson at Faber and Faber.

My friends and family for laughing encouragingly.

Ole Gunnar Solskjær.

Sir Bob Geldof.

Puressence.

There are some excellent websites if your anagram appetite has been whetted.
www.wordsmith.org, www.anagramgenius.com and www.anagrammy.com are all worth a visit and contain some extraordinary examples of word wizardry.

Mini Teletext Hunt,
A Rich Randi Rep